Air-Raid Shelters
of World War II

To my mother and father: Joyce who lived through it, and
Albert, who was a stoker on minesweepers

Air-Raid Shelters
of World War II

Family Stories of Survival in the Blitz

Stephen Wade

REMEMBER WHEN

First published in Great Britain in 2011 by
Remember When
an imprint of
Pen & Sword Books Ltd
47 Church Street
Barnsley
South Yorkshire
S70 2AS

ISBN 978-1-84884-327-1

Typeset in 11pt Ehrhardt by
Mac Style, Beverley, E. Yorkshire

Printed and bound in the UK by the MPG Books Group

Pen & Sword Books Ltd incorporates the imprints of Pen & Sword
Aviation, Pen & Sword Maritime, Pen & Sword Military, Wharncliffe
Local History, Pen and Sword Select, Pen and Sword Military Classics and
Leo Cooper.

For a complete list of Pen & Sword titles please contact
PEN & SWORD BOOKS LIMITED
47 Church Street, Barnsley, South Yorkshire, S70 2AS, England
E-mail: enquiries@pen-and-sword.co.uk
Website: www.pen-and-sword.co.uk

Contents

Introduction

The sisters had been out for a night at the pictures, and had been sitting in the Malvern cinema, in Beeston, Leeds, forgetting all about the war raging around them outside. But on the way home, just three streets away, Joyce and Audrey heard the wail of the sirens. Home and the coal cellar were too far away, so they darted into the nearest shelter they knew. Inside, a dozen regulars were cosily entrenched in the safe little womb of the shelter, and their faces stared at the two strangers. Such was the unwelcome expression on the faces that the sisters sat in silence, and kept quiet even as the others started their community sing-song.

This was an uncommon experience in the years of the Blitz during the Second World War. The normal situation was that the shelters brought people together, overcame the British reserve and created a positive community spirit, bringing a crucially important element to the circumstances. Some were made from spaces already in existence and some were regulation size; others were made from all kinds of improvised building, while others were simply adaptations of related buildings. The singing and the chats, the stories and the jokes were more common than the 'them and us' of British class and status.

Hitler and his *Luftwaffe* thought that little England would cave in, and that the people, scurrying like rats underground, would be happy to accept defeat and be part of the new Third Reich. How wrong the Führer was. Fortress England did not give in.

When we look back at those years, from the first Blitz of 1940 to the doodlebugs near the end of the conflict, we marvel at the toughness and resilience of the ordinary British people. Survival became an art and a skill, learned the hard way through fear and desperation, but it worked and the war was won. It was a time of digging, darkness, ration books, paranoia about loose talk and fear of death. But the war years confirmed the general opinion of the rest of the world that the British were too dogged and stubborn to even dream of the possibility of defeat.

The sheer strength of the population impresses more than many other comparative scenarios in history. Through the centuries there have been extended sieges; there have been die-hard stiff upper lip refusals to bend and submit. There have been extreme sufferings and almost intolerable wartime confrontations, but few can claim to equal the Nazi assault on the cities of Britain. Casualties came from far more than the bombings; danger lurked in the blackout. On top of that there were the evacuations of children, the billeting of bomb victims in other houses, and beneath all this there was the universal but often suppressed feeling that the present day might be your last on earth.

London had known bombs before: 158 Londoners had died in the daytime raid in June, 1917. A school in Poplar had been hit, with the loss of eighteen young lives. The Great War brought 600 deaths in London alone from air-raids. But in the inter-war years news of bombings had been few and far between, notable events being the bombing of Guernica in the Spanish Civil War and the Italian bombing of Ethiopia as Mussolini sought to extend his empire.

The years after the Second World War raids meant that historians worked to assess the significance of certain places and specific bombings, but nothing will ever efface the dark memories of the raids on London, Liverpool, Coventry, Sheffield and Hull in the first phase and Bath in the later phase. The memories, anecdotes and images from those terrible attacks have been part of several oral history projects, notably the BBC storehouse online, and also of local historians' efforts to keep the events in the area of past time which we must reserve for regular revisitations, just as we do for Armistice Day. The story of the Blitz is, above all else, an oral history from the people: a story as gripping, dramatic and horrendous as anything the nineteenth-century ordeals of the working classes under duress can give. But it is still something that will slip away with time, as even the most significant slices of history will do, if memory is not renewed. This book is one contribution to that effort of preservation.

Yet 'preservation' is a dead word. The aim is to keep the stories alive. In preparation for the book, I appealed for stories and memories and pictures in all kinds of publications, and the response was overwhelming. As may be seen from my thanks and acknowledgements at the end of the book, none of my projects have ever involved so much help from people. Without their contributions this book would never have been written.

The truth is that we are doing those wartime heroes proud. We stage exhibitions, publish memorial booklets and dress up in forties' clothes. In Hemswell, Lincolnshire, there is a former RAF base which is now used as an antique centre, and within one of the ex-forces buildings there is a café devoted entirely to the Second World War lifestyle. The visitor steps into 1940, surrounded by music of the time and by artefacts of all kinds; he can pick up a magazine of that period or even read a copy of a contemporary newspaper.

In October 2009, Stockport hosted a special event with air-raid shelters in mind. Matt Davis reported: 'A special event entitled "Standing Together: Remembering the Home Front" was held in the shelters and Stockport market to mark the opening of the network of tunnels on October 28, 1939 which kept townsfolk safe during the bombing raids.' Visitors also learned how gas masks were fitted, and two actors, Gert and Daisy, were in costume, providing memories and tales of the Blitz.

However, nostalgia is one thing: the actual horror of bombing is something else entirely. Harry Wilmot, who was in Bow Common, recalled an image of the most terrible aspect of that time:

Whole streets had been destroyed. All through Sunday and Monday East Enders drifted miserably westwards, looking for shelters: most of them had no baggage; they had lost everything; some carried pathetic and clumsy bundles of their remaining belongings...They had nowhere to rest, nowhere to wash...

Sometimes a memory encapsulates the whole trajectory of the experience, as in this account from Mr D A Palmer of Sheffield:

I was 6 years old in 1939. Before going in the Army, my father and other adults constructed the air-raid (Anderson) shelter, digging a roughly 8ft by 6ft hole. The shelter came in about a dozen pieces, some curved with nuts and bolts to keep it in place. Our shelter at first was often flooded. But they put in some drains in 1940–41. My father, in the Army, left my mother, three sisters and me to occupy the shelter on many nights, as Sheffield was heavily bombed.

We very often went in the shelter around 6 p.m. and came to the all-clear siren around 7 in the morning, when the adults went to work and the kids to school. Bunks were issued after a while to make things a little more comfortable. We lived around 3 miles out of Sheffield city centre, which was very much destroyed, and most of the bombing was aimed at the steel works, which was around the same distance from where we lived. At various times we had gas scares and we went in the shelter in Wellingtons and what waterproofs we had, and in the winter as many clothes as we could get on as it was freezing cold. Over the war years the shelters took on bombs, land mines, buzz bombs with engines that cut out.

Also, as we were surrounded by ack-ack guns and barrage balloons, lots of shrapnel was flying about, which us kids loved to search for after a raid. Anderson shelters must have saved thousands of lives.

Mr Palmer has given us here all the essential features of life with a shelter. As my story goes on, these experiences will recur. But the main point here is that the shelters had to be lived in for a considerable period: they were, in many senses, habitations in which time stopped, places in which people existed in a sort of uncanny and displaced limbo, outside all routine. That gap of time had to be filled, and the experiences inside the shelters will form a major part of this story.

As for my personal memories, some explanation of them may help to put things in perspective. I was born in 1948. I still have my ration book for 1953–54. The family photographs show my father as a naval rating heading off for Malta. Several uncles fought in the war, serving as engineers in the RAF or as able seamen. One uncle fought as a Chindit in Burma. As a child I heard the stories. Uncle Bill was there when the Italians strung up Mussolini. But tales from the Home Front were more readily forthcoming; the servicemen themselves wanted to forget it all and get back to normality, with hard work, young families and summer weeks spent at Blackpool or Filey. The Home Front came to me in the form of tales of Granddad Joe Schofield, ARP in Leeds but also shunted down to London where his bricklaying skills were needed in shoring up and repairing when possible.

I had the stories in the form of amusing memories: Aunty Grace bumping into a pole in the blackout; the taste of a pear from a boyfriend when such treats were rare; girls taken out by Italian POWs, and then the stories from the shelter. These were both shocking and funny, as tragicomedy tends to emerge after the passage of time. The most typical concerns the shelter in Beeston – merely the two cellars beneath the massive terraced house in South Ridge Street – and the story is about the removal of a grate cover by workmen. The cover was taken but not replaced. Then during a blackout a man fell through, falling into my Granddad's coal cellar which was next to the shelter cellar where the family sat. During this raid, they had gathered there and the poor man who fell through walked into their shelter black and wounded – a figure from a nightmare who turned out to be a sad casualty of the raid and the darkness.

It was all mythic to me when first I heard the tales. But somehow I always felt a part of it, because I had that ration book. I just knew that it was so momentous, the war and the scale of the effort to win through, that I needed to feel a tiny part of it all, even though I had been conceived soon after the last triumphal celebrations. Such is the power of the narrative which is created when a family story meets and enhances a national story. Time does erase the pain of course, and has a tendency to make rose-tinted spectacles with which to look at it. 'Black Saturday' – 7 September, 1940 – will surely never be 'rosy'. But despite the horrendous statistics of 13,000 dead by the end of 1940, memories of the later period, when habits of self-preservation mixed with stern stoicism and obdurate humour, the spirit of communal togetherness had won through. The survival strategies led to a thousand different tales of coping and adapting, such as the habit of walking in the blackout in a line across the road, holding hands, so that the people at the ends of the line, when falling into a ditch, could be hauled up by friends. That is a typical story from the time, an account of a coping strategy and sheer brilliant lateral thinking.

The doodlebug (V1) campaign of June to September, 1944 is now something we consider with a dark ironic gloom, because with hindsight we know that the Nazi war scientists were busy, as Hitler was hemmed in and in retreat, creating lethal new models such as the 'People's Flight' and other innovative aerial killing machines. Thank God these came too late to make more mayhem and mass murder across the Channel. Instead of those dire consequences and in spite of the deaths by doodlebug (5,000 people), the stories of hiding from this monstrosity tend to be light-hearted. By that date, acceptance had become a habit.

How does one set about gathering information about such a period in history? After all, the subject is a discrete, self-contained area of enquiry. Yet the difficulty lies in the fact that it has almost become a parody of itself – this in the sense that because anyone can roughly imagine a smallish underground cave-like place with a family huddled around sandwiches and cocoa, that would be the general impression. How wrong can one be! The truth is that people, in their thousands, were cowering and shivering in miserable surroundings, wondering if they were going to die that night.

With this in mind, I set about asking for stories. There were three phases in this: first a review of what was in print already. That consists of a mix of memoirs in small print publications and large, comprehensive books on the war in general. Second came letters to local and regional newspapers asking for memoirs, pictures and anecdotes. Finally there were the academic sources, in journals and periodicals. Of all these sources, the most surprising was the massive and enthusiastic response I had from people who had read my appeal for stories. It was overwhelming; the feeling I had must be similar to that of a man who asks universal questions such as 'What's it like to have a baby?' Thousands of women could answer that question: many would say virtually the same thing, but others would have had unique experiences; some would have gone through agony and others would tell their tale with a smile.

That is what happened with my appeal. The contrasts were sharp: some told stories of having a laugh or singing the latest hit song; others spoke of unimaginable pain and loss. This was one episode in a war which spanned the globe; most respondents would have had relatives somewhere across the world, in a Burmese jungle or in a platoon trekking across the desert. They were part of an epic story, and every action in the struggle was part of a huge, almost infinite string of actions that formed a network, and that network was called 'The World War'. What must be accepted is that my respondents were mostly in their eighties. That means that they were children or young people in the Blitz. To them the notion of a 'world war' was known, if at all, simply from their fathers' stories of the trenches or the Middle East. My mother was born in 1926 and was working as a machinist in 1941, having left school to help add to the family income. Her father, my grandfather Joe Schofield, fought in Mesopotamia (modern-day Iraq) in 1917. He would have realised he was in a world war, but would have, again, simply no idea what the big picture was.

This addition to 'Remember When' will indulge in a little nostalgia, but the oral history I have collected will dominate the story, such are the incredibly poignant tales I have gathered. Some myths may continue, but on the whole, the social history of mass destruction will have another batch of stories for the archives, but those stories will also live on the following pages.

Prelude: A Scenario

It has been a cloudy, chilly evening. Mother is baking jam tarts and apple pie. Dad is not there: he is in Europe somewhere, but his face looks out at her from the little black and white photo on the mantelpiece. From the Bakelite radio, a dance band plays and Al Bowlly sings softly, of romance, candlelight and wine. The dog snores on the hearth-rug, a furnishing made of strips of old cloth looped into a hessian rectangle.

It is early spring 1940 and Mother likes to imagine that there is no war; that everything is as it used to be. That Tom would come home from his park gardening job at six; that they would go out for a pint and a gin and tonic at the Malt Shovel and talk about the summer holiday at the seaside.

Young Billy is at the pictures with the girl from number eighteen and they are going steady. Mother looks up from her kitchen table which is covered with flour, puts down the rolling pin and stares wistfully out into the dusk across the garden. She can just make out the mound of the Anderson shelter. 'Oh no … the food and the drinks!' She rushes across the kitchen and boils a kettle, then fills a flask with tea. Next she sets about making cheese and salad sandwiches and puts these in a bag, along with some lemonade.

When all this is done, she is about to return to her baking but glances at the clock. 'If it's going to start it should be in about an hour,' she thinks. Strange, but it is almost routine. She walks to the back door. The dog gets a scent of cold air and walks to her, brushing against her stockinged legs. She looks up at the sky, then checks the coats on the hooks on the back door – three warm coats ready to put on before they scuttle out to the shelter – Grandma, Billy and herself. Or maybe Audrey will come with them – she's almost a daughter-in-law, after all …

They will be laughing now at the Ritz cinema; chuckling at some Laurel and Hardy antics, perhaps. But then she looks at the sky again and she imagines that sight: the rows of planes like malevolent dark crows, bringing a ripple of fear into her veins. Yet she doesn't feel a tear or feel sad in any way. On the contrary, she looks again at the row of coats, then strokes the bag of food and drink and smiles, almost contentedly. 'It's like the tree-house,' she thinks. 'Just like running out to hide in the tree-house ... but I wanted to be up there. This time I'm going to sit with my feet in water ...'

She laughs to herself, and then the laugh bursts into the kind of chortle she made as a schoolgirl. She laughs and laughs until she sobs and goes to grab the photo of her lost son Arthur and then hugs it to her breast.

Chapter 1

1939: Andersons and Morrisons

'Steel air-raid shelters, now in course of manufacture, intended for the protection of persons living in non-basement houses, today received their "baptism of fire ..."'

The Times, 14 February 1939

On Monday, 4 September, 1939, *The Daily Telegraph* headline announced: 'Great Britain at War'. The list of statements before the leading article were on the King's message to the Empire, the creation of the War Cabinet and the news that Winston Churchill was to be First Lord of the Admiralty. The crux of the news was plain and direct: 'The Prime Minister announced yesterday morning in a message broadcast to Britain, that as from 11 o'clock in the morning, Great Britain was at war with Germany.'

In spite of Neville Chamberlain's famous arrival from talks with Adolf Hitler and his piece of paper, reinforced by his assurance that he had achieved 'peace in our time', the general feeling had been, for some considerable time, that war was inevitable. On page 5 of that issue, Chamberlin Weatherstraps Ltd were selling their gas protection, in response to a booklet produced by the Home Office called *The Protection of Your Home Against Air-Raids*. The sales talk was ambiguous: 'Originally designed for peacetime comfort, this equipment has now assumed an added value in so far that whilst minimising the infiltration of a current of air, it minimises in the same proportion the infiltration of POISON GAS carried by that current.' Readers were asked to believe that such a product had been in demand in peacetime.

The unreal and uneasy period called 'The Phoney War' had now begun. The term was used by American writers, noting the stand-off with regard to Poland, which had been invaded and easily taken by the Nazis. But within that period, the Home Front was all about the expectation that the bombers would be coming. In terms of propaganda, much was said about the relative merits of the *Luftwaffe* and the RAF of course; Hermann Goering had proudly shown off his air force at a number of displays and special occasions, so the RAF had a point to prove. It was hard to believe that Britain and her fighter planes were ready, and therefore the mindset of being bombed was created, and measures began, at speed, to prepare for the worst.

Predictions were dire. Early casualties on the offensive fronts must have led to more feelings of a dismal outcome: 600 men had been killed in the first two weeks of conflict. Still, one thing had been instilled into the British mind, famously by Baden-Powell: 'Be prepared.' There is no doubt that in terms of shelters, that was the case. In January 1939, the Air Raid Precautions Department at the Home Office had been liaising with the steel industry to produce shelters, and the Lord Privy Seal, Sir John Anderson, announced that shelters would be provided for the people in small houses, against blasts and splinters, and debris from adjacent buildings.

The Times announced, 'An initial order for 120,000 tons of steel sheets, channels and accessories sufficient to make 400,000 "unit shelters" has been placed. Further orders will follow as the productive capacity of industry comes into full play.' In tandem with these measures, the London Fire Brigade was being organised, under the command of Commander Firebrace, and this was to be the first stage of a national plan to streamline the process of readiness when the raids came.

The tone of the newspaper information was that matters had been very carefully thought out. The legendary German organisation and efficiency was possible for a nation which had run a massive empire, and the official language was very persuasive, suggesting a confidence which was so essential in the circumstances: 'The shelters will be supplied in sections, making up complete units capable of giving protection to four or five persons.' Everything about the dissemination of the information was smooth and plain: 'Distribution to the households will be undertaken by a special organisation which is being set up by the railway companies. The Home Office will pay the railway companies the cost of distribution.'

The Brains Involved

Several talented people worked on the design of shelters. John Sommerfield, ironically a man born in Berlin in 1913 whose real Christian names were Kurt Joachim, was at first involved in the work. But he attained fame at a high level when he invented a revolutionary system of producing a portable roadway capable of carrying heavy vehicles. On the invasion beaches when the Allies hit back at Hitler, this was used to provide traction for tanks, amphibious vehicles and lorries. It was also invaluable for movement of transport in the desert campaigns. Had he stayed on shelter work, there could have been another alternative to the famous Anderson, but we will never know.

The Anderson Shelter

This garden shelter was designed by William Paterson and three other engineers also worked on it, including Oscar Kerrison. But it took its name from Sir John Anderson. It was a simple concept: two curved sides of corrugated steel were placed in a deep pit, and then earth to a depth of at least 15 inches was placed on top. They were meant to house six people. Six of the panels were bolted together and there was a drainage sump. The height was 6 feet and they were 4 feet 6 inches wide.

William Paterson was born in Roslin in 1874, and educated in Edinburgh, training at the Heriot-Watt College there. He served an apprenticeship of six years before working for a firm of paper mill engineers. He formed his own water purification company in 1902. He filed over seventy patents in his long career, but it was in 1939 that he came into his own, when Sir John Anderson asked him to devise a shelter. The stipulation was that the construction had to withstand blast and flying debris, but had to be such that models could be made rapidly. The rest is history. He was knighted in 1944 for his success in conceiving the 'Anderson' and surely must have felt that the shelter should have been known to history as a 'Paterson'.

By 2 February, the information was about compulsory ARP shelters. Sir John Anderson had prepared a white paper and his recommendation was that there should be provision for shelters in several types of building. This imposed regulations on employers to provide shelters and made grants available for half the cost involved. The steel Anderson shelters were to be given free to the poorer citizens; readers were reassured that directions would be given as to where to build shelters and how to follow the right procedure. Anderson had also given much thought to the issue of strengthening basements and for making commercial shelters. Later that month a means test was announced.

Organisation required

Authorities were asked to provide lists of people who were eligible for free shelters; some cities and towns were placed on a priority list for the first deliveries. The key statement was:

> The Government have decided that the distribution of these shelters shall be made in the first place to householders in types of houses for which they are designed who cannot be expected to pay for them. Such persons may be defined as follows: persons whose occupations are compulsorily insurable under the National Health Insurance Act and persons not compulsorily insured … who are mainly dependent on earnings (or pension) not exceeding £250. This amount to be increased by £50 for each child of school age in excess of two.

Sir John Anderson received a flood of other ideas and suggestions for shelters, as various interested parties realised that there would be a need for shelters tailor-made to the location of their use. Anderson responded by pointing out that:

> The main purpose of protection must be reconciled with the paramount necessity of maintaining the productive efficiency of the nation in time of war … This involves important psychological considerations as well as considerations of air strategy which are necessarily outside common knowledge and cannot be fully ventilated in public.

It was pointed out in various quarters that panic would be the cause of a number of deaths and could also spoil the best-laid plans. For instance, the Mersey Tunnel, clearly a very useful place to run when the sirens sounded, was 'rejected as a shelter by responsible local opinion' according to *The Times*. By February, decisions on provision were expected. What was needed was testing, and that took place at Shoeburyness in February. The press carried a sequence of photos showing the testing, from a shot of three officers standing by a bomb to the trial of steel against high explosive. *The Times* reported: 'Today's test was to demonstrate as nearly as possible the effect of a high explosive bomb when dropped in close proximity to the new shelters in typical war conditions.' A brick building was made, to copy the shape of a row of cottages; the walls were 18 inches thick, and two steel shelters were put in front of them. These were 6ft 6in. by 4ft 6in., made of straight and curved corrugated iron sheets, one-tenth of an inch thick. Between the brick building and the shelters a 500lb bomb was placed with its nose buried in the ground, simulating a dropped bomb. The effect of the explosion was that there was thick smoke and from that it was noted that bricks and wood were thrown 100 feet into the air. The cottage-type buildings were obliterated and a crater was left measuring 17 feet across and 6 feet in depth. What of the shelter?

The shelter only had a dusting of brick pieces. The report at the time commented: 'The sight of the shelters absolutely intact was all the more impressive as one viewed the havoc wrought in the structure or gazed into the crater formed by the explosion.' The reporter also noted that, as he drove away from Shoeburyness, he saw a shelter in a private garden being inspected.

Naturally, there was comment and response, and people knew about the fairly recent experience of bombing in Spain, so that was a point of reference. A M Rouse, Chief Technical Adviser to the ARP Department at the Home Office, wrote to the press with this contribution, after some scaremongering by a Mr Helsby:

The bomb used in the Shoeburyness test and the depth at which it was detonated, with its nose 18in. below the ground, were chosen with the view of demonstrating the effects which could be expected with the explosion of a bomb most likely to be directed against civil buildings. Mr Helsby states that in Barcelona the blast of bombs frequently sheared the kerbstone at the gutter level. This would be from bombs falling on a hard road surface. The steel air-raid shelters which are being issued to the public ... will be situated in gardens, where they will be surrounded by soft earth.

Everything in print relating to shelters was couched in terms of extreme reassurance, of course. Mr Helsby was well-known to Mr Rouse and they had discussed a report on Barcelona, but Helsby apparently wanted his moment of fame in the press.

But what about the work involved in the Anderson shelter? John Perry recalls the arrival and emplacement:

Being born in 1932 I can remember the Anderson air-raid shelters being delivered to most of the houses in Watford, Herts, where I then lived. I can still see those sheets of very thick gauge steel with the characteristic curve at one end. Those pieces then had to be assembled and dug into the ground, which required a very large hole being excavated. After the excavation soil had to be put onto the top to lessen the effects of blast. They made a good piece of garden to grow marrows. I do not remember a door being provided; I seem to think of most people's shelters with a door of old carpet or sacking.

David Carney of Rotherham also remembers the delivery of the Anderson shelter. He writes:

It was assembled by my father who then dug the hole for it in the garden. It was our refuge at the time of the Sheffield raids. After the war it was downgraded to a junk store with rockery flowers growing over the top of the earth mound. It finally went for scrap. All signs that it ever existed were obliterated.

David has been moved to immortalise the shelter in verse:

ANDERSON

Corrugated curves and straights,
Nuts and bolts, angle plates.
Amateur assembly hurried,
Deep-set in the garden buried.
Sirens wailing, helter-skelter,
Place of refuge, air-raid shelter.

Double bunks and condensation;
Mum and dad and old relation
Crammed together for the night
Gripping every child's hand tight.
Bated breath and hearts that stop
Waiting for the bomb to drop.

Rusting relic now used for
Junk and dad's old bike to store.
Rockery now growing well
On that mound where shrapnel fell.
Soon all trace will disappear.
Garden once again 'All Clear'.

By the end of 1939 it was clear that there were four main categories of shelter: the Anderson, dug into the earth; then came the Morrison, along with the basement one which was knocked through so that bombed neighbours could move through to other caverns, and finally the public or communal one, including the Tube and other subterranean ones across the land.

Responses were mixed. E R Chamberlain reported one man from London saying:

Proper death traps they are in my opinion. A pal of mine over in Islington way has turned his upside down and used it as a duck pond – and that's about the best thing you can do with them – wouldn't get me in one of those things.

In the end, around 27 per cent of the population used them.

In Leeds, on 4 September 1939, people got cracking, ready to protect themselves. The first siren sounded and people were surprisingly calm. But many had started digging the trenches ready for the shelters; public shelters had been arranged but there were complaints that entrances to these had been blocked by people sitting too close to the doors, and the problem of smokers already reared up. A no-smoking policy for shelters was advocated by the more vociferous citizens. The Council wanted to build around eighty shelters within a half-mile radius of the city centre.

Basements were soon converted for use, such as the one beneath the famous Grand Theatre, and then others were made on Vicar Lane and at York Road.

In Grimsby, the new Andersons created more of a stir. They were put on display and some borough council workmen assembled one on Ainslie Street Recreation Ground to show people how it was done. The usual mass of printed information followed. There is no doubt that the Council were forward-thinking: they had a list of builders who were to be engaged to make supplementary shelters – these were more expensive, but there would have certainly been buyers for them. The paperwork suggested that there would be between 15,000 and 16,000 shelters needed. But all this led to disappointment because the problem was with the water beneath. The water table was too high, as it was in Hull, and so after sinking the trenches, water seeped in. Flooding was a major problem, and the answer was clearly going to be that public shelters made more sense.

A feature on the *This is Grimsby* website explains what happened next:

> The Council reported that large numbers were still waiting for work to start while many people 'had made no effort to comply with regulations' and had simply put the shelter up in their back gardens, with no thought to 'the requisite cover of earth, position or method of erection'.

But soon war was declared and things accelerated: 'There was frantic activity...with Anderson shelters springing up everywhere. Elsewhere, fifteen of the brick and concrete communal shelters were under construction.'

The Morrison Shelter

The Morrison shelter was described to me by Valerie Rowan:

> We were allocated a Morrison shelter which looked like a large metal rabbit hutch; it was given to people with small houses or bungalows and ours doubled up as our parents' bed. Some people, including our neighbours, used it as the top of a dining table. When the dreaded siren sounded we all used to rush to the shelter, packing in as best we could. My Mother's mother, known to us as Grandma, was staying with us (her house was let to evacuees) and came into the shelter with us – it was quite a squash.
>
> There were three adults and two children, of which I was one. I used to make sure my little pet terrier Frisky, was in...Soon Grandma began to complain: 'That dog smells AWFUL – push him out!' I protested, 'But he might get bombed.' Grandma got up and departed quickly, saying, 'I'll get out then, I'd rather be bombed than gassed...'

Valerie's father was frightened that, as he could only manage to get half of his body inside, he would be split in two if there was a direct hit.

A room interior showing a Morrison shelter. (*Lincolnshire Archives Local Studies Collection*)

The Morrison was provided when it was realised that there was a need for an indoor shelter; Herbert Morrison was Home Secretary and also Minister for Home Security, and the shelter with his name was issued by March 1941. It was a long table with mesh sides and a steel top. It was only 2 feet 6 inches high, and 6 feet 6 inches long. It was obtained if purchased at a cost of £7 12s 6d, but was free to low-income families.

Digging and Planning

In February 1939 the question of camouflaging the shelter took centre stage. There had been digging in public parks, done without planning, and these were an eyesore. Appeals were made to 'the art of the gardener' to put this right. On 16 February, a firm from Surrey staged a demonstration in London, and *The Times* reported:

A section of trenches typical of those to be seen in London parks today formed part of a model, while the other part presented a pleasant garden design which could be used effectively to hide trenches ... there was a particularly attractive design, called the Garden of Peace, intended to conceal a private shelter, consisting of a rose garden with sundial screened by yew hedges.

'Home Sweet Home' – making your shelter a fit place to live in! (*Author's collection*)

An item from a 1939 gardening catalogue shows a flat-capped pensioner hammering at a wooden frame at the entrance of his distinctive garden shelter. He has made diamond-shaped side windows with tiled corners and also added a step at the entrance to match, giving the building a Mediterranean look. At each side of his door there are small beds with flowers and lights. Above the shelter, the roof is covered in various high plants.

In her mansion above Torbay, aged millionaire Mrs Ella Rowcroft had 'the finest air-raid shelter in the country' constructed. But she died before it could be used. Susan Briggs wrote that a lift took her down below the ground to a depth of 30 feet, to a long corridor with rooms leading off it. In Mrs Rowcroft's bedroom there was a bronze plate with the words, 'Angels are watching overhead. Sleep sweetly then, Goodnight.'

So enthusiastic were the gardening British to adorn their shelters that one reporter at the time told his readers in America that 'there was a greater danger of being hit by a vegetable marrow falling off the roof of an air-raid shelter than of being struck by a bomb'. The British skill of creating cosiness was everywhere evident. Geoffrey Smith was 8 when war broke out. He recalls the general amicability around him:

The soldiers on the searchlight became family friends, except many failed to return from France after D-Day. Their accommodation on site was simple wooden huts. The guy manning the diesel generator (no pun intended – he was called Joe Manning) had his own little hut next to the machine, complete with table, chair and bunk bed, ready for action within a minute's notice. One of them composed a little rhyme beginning,

> *I am one of the searchlight crew*
> *I'm browned off because I have nothing to do ...*

The shelters, the ARP post and the gun emplacements all became sites of cosy domestic comfort, as much as that could be achieved with effort. It was ingrained in the British mind to do that, to make efforts towards domestication and as much comfort as possible. It was the same approach which had made 'homes' of bunkers in the trench systems of the Western Front in the Great War. It is one of the ironies of modern history that the Germans have a word for that attitude and situation: *Gemütlichkeit*. The nearest we have is 'homely'.

There was the challenge of making the shelter as well. In 1938 the Government had issued a clear and detailed leaflet with visual instructions on trenching and shelter construction. In some places this was a communal task, as one memory notes:

> I can remember my father digging a huge hole in the back garden with help from neighbours, and putting an Anderson shelter into it, covering it all up and putting a strawberry bed on top. There were steps down to the shelter and dad had put bench seats all round. These places were designated for each of the neighbours: Mrs Boot, Mrs Bradburn, Nanny Cliffe and Mr Cliffe and of course mum and dad. Dad himself was a first-aid warden and was always on duty when the sirens went.

The instructions from 1938 began with a trench with required depths indicated, then the sequence of work was like this if you wanted a top-notch one; many were happy to make the simpler version, of course.

Constructing an Anderson Shelter

<u>Digging Main Trench with A and B sections</u>
One man, four hours. (To a depth of 6 feet)

<u>Revetting Trench</u>
Corrugated iron sides and wooden trench supports in place
(protection space for six people)

<u>Finished Trench</u>
Anchor pegs fixed at ends; duck boards or cinders at base;
Tar or creosoted supports and a covered, gas-proof entrance curtain

---

The leaflet and its pictures create a formidable challenge.

Sometimes, because there was so much supervision and regulation, householders did not quite plan and construct in a suitable way. J Walsh, for instance, remembers the arrival and the later changes:

> I was 8 when the war started and I can remember the authorities delivering Anderson shelters to each household. A bag of nuts and

Wally Thompson, a riveter at the dock, erecting an Anderson shelter in his garden. (*Lincolnshire Archives Local Studies Collection*)

curved washers and a spanner were included with the galvanised corrugated steel parts of the shelter. An instruction sheet was included. The shelter was assembled in a 3-foot deep hole close to the back door of the house, and covered with soil… Later we were told to move the shelter to the bottom of the garden as the shelter would be covered with debris if the house was hit. Sandbags were provided to build a blast wall at the front of the shelter to protect the door.

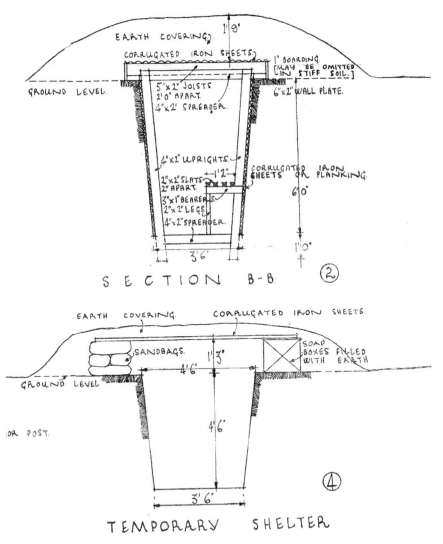

'If the Invader Comes', a leaflet of an alarmist nature. (*Courtesy of Derek Sprake*)

Derek Sprake, a writer from the Isle of Wight, has given an account of his family's trenching work:

> My father and grandfather built one of these trenches in a field they owned next to our house. The field was higher than the road and they made their entrance through the bank, so that the entrance was at road level, but the trench was below ground level, although the roof did stand above. My understanding was that they made the inside as comfortable as possible with a mattress to lay on. They, with my grandmother … spent one night in the shelter to 'test it out' but found it too damp and uncomfortable and they never entered it again!

In fact, Derek adds that later, when some cows were allowed to graze in that field, they went on the roof and it fell in.

Naturally, communal shelters also appeared or were made, adapted or commandeered, depending on the space and the location. Top of the list was the London Underground. The Tube became such an important part of the shelter provision that it generated an oral history of its own. The subterranean world of the raids included tunnels, basements beneath hotels and the train routes. But there was a fear that a 'deep shelter mentality' would emerge, and that mobility would be affected. Typical of the provision was the half-mile of disused tunnel beneath

GARDEN TRENCH SHELTER 1

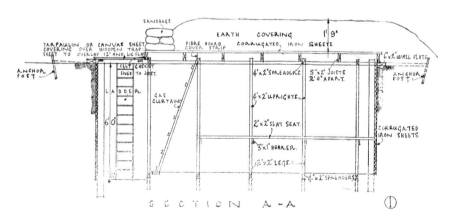

A trench design. (*Courtesy of Derek Sprake*)

Borough High Street in London, which held 8,000 people. A further 12,000 people could be accommodated at Finsbury Park and 8,000 at King's Cross.

Forget Normal Life

In 1939, though, it was all a matter of normality and family life being totally revolutionised. After the declaration of war, everything that had been theorised and speculated upon suddenly became either urgent or useless, as exigencies made clear the actions to be taken. After all, there had been measures taken with regard to bombing as early as January 1938, when workmen in Leicester, for instance, painted kerbstones white as part of a blackout trial. It was time for propaganda and communications to play their part, as the Government realised that enduring a certain bombing campaign was as much a psychological war as a public, military one. The media went to work: cartoons were generated, leaflets were produced; the papers did everything they could to inform and also to instil the sense of the British stiff upper lip. People would have to face all the secondary effects of the bombing, and the priority was the safety of the children. Evacuation began, and the scale of this, and the sheer complexity of the movement of people, is staggering when we look back today.

The evacuation in September 1939 transported 660,000 women and children out to rural areas: that figure is the official one, and there were definitely many more moved in other channels. London's civilian population dropped by 43 per cent in two years, between 1939 and 1941. As children stood on railway platforms huddled in groups, and with tickets tied to their clothes stating their name, school and number, their parents must have been terrified that a last goodbye was imminent. *The Daily Telegraph* claimed that three million had been evacuated, with this statement: 'By tonight [4 September] it is expected that three million children, mothers, blind persons, expectant mothers and cripples will have been billeted in new homes in the country and at the seaside.'

It was going to be a case of adapt and survive, though some were less concerned about the bombing than others. Betty Hughes, from Port Talbot, left her home to help with the war effort in London; she was based at the Charing Cross Hotel, and there she served drinks to American servicemen. She put in some long hours, and when there was a raid she tended to have a little of what today we would call 'me time' rather than go all the way to the basement shelter. She was later to tell

Geoff Gwillian that 'The bloody Germans couldn't get me into a shelter.' But on one occasion of a raid she had decided to have a bath. As she relaxed there, a bomb hit the place and her bedroom was destroyed. All her clothes were gone, and she simply had her bathrobe, towel and cosmetics bag. Amazingly, she received £40 in compensation under the War Damage Act of 1941. Geoff Gwillian concludes his story (now displayed in the hotel) with her happy marriage: 'She had not yet met my uncle Albert Barnes, who was serving in the RAF some time earlier, and they were married in Caxton Hall.'

As Londoners waited with bated breath after gathering around the radio to hear that they were at war, the boltholes were ready, and so was their mindset of resilience and sheer doggedness. As David Hicks from Sheffield wrote in an article in 2009, the words in the air were 'We're all on the front line now!'

Overall, the business of making or adapting spaces for shelter was destined to be well organised, but it has to be said that the attitudes of the public were mixed. Some thought that their neck of the woods would never be a target; others thought that sheds, cupboards and various 'dens' would be fine; some merely thought of the solid double bed in the master bedroom as the best place to hide. Others fashioned their own shelters, with that DIY enterprise many craftsmen and handymen were proud of. Whatever moves were made, at least they were made – very few were complacent. Plenty of veterans from the Great War were skilled with a shovel and knew all about 'digging in' and of course making trenches was really, for many, one of the essential tasks in maintaining an allotment.

Gardeners of Britain were about to be very busy, trying to follow diagrammatic instructions on leaflets or in books. The press sprang into action and made sure that Andersons were the talk of the day. Those people who felt the thrill of life under canvas felt the same adventurous urges at the thought of a den out at the end of the garden. But of course, unlike time spent on jamboree with the Scouts and Guides, this time there were people up there who wanted to drop bombs on you.

Chapter 2

The Blitz and the First Shelter Experience

'I take this bombing as a good sign – the last kick of a drowning man. Hitler wouldn't have done it if he hadn't been up against it.'

J L Hodson

It was an organisational nightmare: how to get thousands upon thousands of shelters made, distributed and of course, understood and accepted. Those who had been to Spain to fight for freedom against Franco had seen what bombing raids were like and they had known a war waged against civilians. They were only too happy to share this experience but that knowledge was also an acceleration of fear. As with all wars, half the apprehension and unease comes as much from not knowing as from actually seeing the enemy.

However, Britain in the 1930s was becoming rather good at organising things. It was an age of administrators. Because the civil servants, statisticians and fact-lovers were so ubiquitous, the result was of course that fear increased. The possibility of invasion was in the air in 1939 and the writers spoke of the Armada and the Channel, and how history had shown that geography was on our side. But Hitler was skilful at invading people, as he had taken several states around his frightening new Third Reich without so much as a by-your-leave, and no-one had tried to stop him. The poet W H Auden saw the flowering of the paranoid anxiety that was growing:

> *O what is that sound which so thrills the ear*
> *Down in the valley, drumming, drumming?*
> *Only the scarlet soldiers dear,*
> *The soldiers coming.*

O what is that light I see flashing so clear
Over the distance, brightly?
Only the sun on their weapons dear,
As they step lightly.

In March 1939 the Austin Motor Company finished its own air-raid protection scheme; this provided deep shelters for around 5,000 workers and created a huge tunnel system close to the Longbridge works. Work had gone forward at a rate of 40 feet per day, making a height of 9 feet and a width of 16 feet 9 inches. On average, the tunnels were over 50 feet below ground level. Applications for steel shelters accelerated: by 11 March, the City of London received over 31,000 applications.

There was also a campaign run by the Cement and Concrete Association for domestic pill-boxes. At a lunch at the Savoy Hotel, Lord Wolmer pointed out that concrete had been used in the construction of the Maginot Line and the Siegfried Line and he said that it could provide 'in every home a miniature Gibraltar which would serve to protect the families of the nation and also maintain the morale of the people'.

In Richmond the bridges were considered as possible shelters; opinion was that the space under the arches of Richmond Bridge was enough to take 1,000 people. The press reported that Twickenham Bridge was being studied with a view to protecting the residents of St. Margaret's and Isleworth, and similarly, the Kingston Bridge was possibly to be used for people in Hampton Wick, and the Hampton Court Bridge for Palace and Molesly folk.

Official Shelters Arrive
The deliveries really took off at the end of February and forty-two wagons of the Great Western Railway travelled from Newport to Acton and then London, bringing shelter components. The Maiden Lane goods depot was used as the central store, and 1,000 shelters had reached there by 24 February. *The Times* made a note of another benefit of the production of shelters:

WORK FOR UNEMPLOYED

In the work of delivery the London, Midland and Scottish Railway Company will use horse-drawn drays, each capable of carrying four shelters ... Householders have the option of accepting the shelters for storage, of erecting them themselves, or having them sunk and erected by the local authority ... Where necessary unemployed workers will be used to assist the council workmen.

In April, the royal family took part in an exercise. An 'attack' from the air was arranged, and a siren sounded; Princess Elizabeth, Princess Margaret and the Duke and Duchess of Kent 'took cover' in a bomb-proof shelter. That was typical of a wide variety of preparatory moves for all kinds of resources and stand-by arrangements.

In the Middle Temple, for instance, the staff and barristers were all trained as ARP personnel, and with water imminently in great need, an old well in Pump Court was put back into use. It held around 3,000 gallons. It was cleaned out and was potentially also useful as a fire-fighting supply.

Another potential location for shelters was car parks. In 1939 there was a method called the Baldwin-Auger system of dual-purpose structures. This was basically an automatic lifting method which allowed for support of the right strength for dual purpose, and so shelter cover was potentially acceptable in between 500 and 600 sites across the country. The system in car parks was that a push-button method brought vehicles up to surface level. The best minds were at work to find ways of preserving cars and other vehicles, and of course the underground space could accommodate people as well.

These and many other lines of thought in terms of preparation and readiness for the expected bombers filled up talk, print and broadcast time for months. But when would the actual raids begin? How would people actually cope? What was expected? There were some official estimates of casualties: one figure quoted was that there would be 58,000 dead in London after the first raid.

It happened on 7 September 1940. This was always to be called 'Black Saturday', for obvious reasons. The *Luftwaffe* had been attacking the airfields in the South, but now the East End was assailed by 337 tons of bombs. Thousands went into the Tube and into other domestic shelters; by the end of the year, there had been 14,000 civilians killed. The bombings spread to other cities: in Coventry, on 14 November, the attack was relentless and terrible.

The artist Edward Ardizzone wrote:

Look at that ... look at that strange, half-ruined street – something terribly moving about it. You know you feel almost like weeping. What was it to do with civilians – that's always hurt me about the war – to do with people who lived in the place?

He saw children dancing and homeless people walking away, smashed by horrendous tragedy. The contrast struck him profoundly, as it did so many.

It was a time of horror and nightmare; imaginations created even more unreal perspectives and horizons. Marilyn Cameron wrote to the *Daily Mail* in 2009, to recall that:

> During night bombing raids we all had to sit in the mud under the corrugated roof ... we saw what appeared to be a gun turret sticking out of the railway embankment ... The air-raid warden was called and we waited terrified until the sun rose ... and the gun turret was revealed as an ancient bush that had been there for years ...

Adapting to the Small Spaces
The new shelters had to become living spaces. It was not enough to see them as places to hide for a few minutes. In the *Daily Sketch* in August 1940, Mary Rose wrote a piece called 'Making the Best of a Sheltered Life' and in that she wrote:

> Some people find it most restful to lie down, and it's a grand idea to put a nice warm rug on the floor if you haven't got a Lilo and there's no room for a small mattress ... Then with two pillows on which to rest your head, you can doze away to your heart's content until the all-clear sounds.

Discomfort had to be overcome first. The sump beneath was usually full of water. Neil Farrell recalls his father really going to town in the cosiness of their shelter:

> Inside ... he dug a sump to collect the ground seepage, and then built a wooden floor with a trapdoor so we could empty the sump as required. It was the children's job to empty it, but we always left some water in to keep our frogspawn and froglets ... Next came the bunk

Shelter in garden. (*Courtesy of Jean Gough*)

beds. Dad built a rack of three on one side of the shelter (we got topped and tailed), a chair for mum to sit in, also steps to get down to the shelter, and he finished it off by running electric out there for lighting and a kettle. I can also remember a large sweet jar with boiled sweets in, to keep the kids quiet during the bombing. If dad was home on leave he would sometimes let us watch the searchlights and dogfights over Liverpool during a raid, from behind the blast wall...

As Neil notes, his dad put in a lot of man hours to keep the family safe. In fact, he says that 'Some nights we would go and sleep in the shelter instead of getting up when the air-raid siren sounded, to make our sleepy way down to the shelter... it was really cosy in there, we loved it.'

Reports of the bombings by mid-September make woeful reading. *The Daily Telegraph* reported on 18 September that:

Noted shops and famous mansions suffered from the bombs which were dropped on the West End on Monday night... By a strange chance, two of the bombs fell close to former residences of the King and Queen. One wrecked a house in Bruton Street only 50 yards from where, as Duke and Duchess of York, they lived when they were first married.

In that raid, a commandant and two headquarters staff at the Women's Legion were killed, reminding readers that, even being in a room beneath a building could not save you from the worst if there was a direct hit, as there had been in this case.

Panic was an enemy created as an offshoot of the bombings. One of the strangest and most extreme panic measures taken was recalled by Peter Langham from Liverpool. He wrote to describe a very alarming happening in Litherland:

> This street, Alton Avenue, was on a slope … air-raid shelters had been dug into all the back gardens so that you had to stoop and go down a couple of steps to enter … my parents told one particular family if there was an air-raid they could share our shelter. In June 1940 at night-time the air-raid siren went, my father was at the docks so my mother told my elder brother to go down the steps ready for me to be handed to him. In the meantime this family of four … rushed up the street into our garden, took me from my mother's arms, threw me into next door's garden, bolted down the steps into the shelter, locked the door and refused to open it until the all-clear sounded.

The tale ends with Peter being found crying among the cabbages.

Watch Out For Folks Selling Materials

In some places it was soon realised that certain undesirable elements would be likely to sell items on the black market. It would be tempting for shady types to help themselves to various possessions and necessities left in the shelter, of course. People were going to be vulnerable in a wartime situation and there were those who would take advantage. In Ireland, for instance, Sean Moylan, Minister for Defence in 1940, issued an order; the main dictates were:

In this order:

1) No person shall sell any article of air-raid precautions equipment unless he is the owner of a licence issued by the Minister under the

next following paragraph authorising him to sell articles of air-raid precautions equipment.

2) The Minister may, whenever and so often as he thinks fit issue to any person a licence authorising such person to sell articles of air-raid precautions equipment, and may attach to any such licence such conditions as he thinks proper.

The subject presented a slight legal quandary in England, as was pointed out in Parliament to poor, beleaguered Sir John Anderson. His name may have become famous, but he was the man to whom all shelter questions were put. The issue here was about legislation that covered such thefts:

Mr T Smith asked the Home Secretary whether he is aware that some local authorities are passing resolutions urging that power should be given to them to proceed against persons who misuse public shelters, and whether he intends to deal with the matter.

Mr Smith : 'Will the Minister keep in mind ... police have hesitated to take out summonses, being of the opinion that there was no Statute under which they could deal with such cases? Will he have enquiries made on this point and if I send him information, will he look into it?'

Anderson certainly did: he was a hard worker and listened to all matters related to shelters.

The first encounter with shelter life was often very unpleasant. Mrs R Lee experienced the Anderson, Morrison and brick communal shelters, and she has a vivid memory of the first bombing:

We had an Anderson shelter in the garden – we only went in it a few times as it filled with water. The first time the sirens went we dashed out in our night clothes all eager to get in before the German planes came over. We found we were up to our knees in water.

The brick shelter was not much better:

We had a brick shelter which was just built in time. As we had quite a lot of nights in the shelter we started to go to bed dressed ready to dash outside, which was really awful in winter time. In 1940 we had a bad

Part of a wall over a ground air-raid shelter showing poor workmanship with gaps between the bricks. (*Lincolnshire Archives Local Studies Collection*)

winter, and we never got any bunks put in the shelter ... not even a door, so us three children and our mother saw and heard everything. On the night of the 12th December we had the Sheffield Blitz. That night and also the 15th December was a heavy bombing raid. We went out in the shelter at 7 p.m. ... and came out at 5.30 a.m. We had nothing to eat or drink. It was bitter cold and we could hardly move as we came out as we just had a few wooden boxes to sit on.

Mrs Lee did indeed have a very tough war. Her father did not come back home. But as she wrote to me: 'After six long years of war, we will be forever grateful for our freedom.'

Sheer Inventiveness

'Making do' became a mindset and a philosophy. Nothing was to be wasted and everything had a use. Refuse collectors had much less to collect and people hoarded. The natural bent for creativity with odds and ends now became a national obsession. Junk in the attic or the cellar was studied for its potential usefulness under fire or as a weapon. Just as the

Home Guard improvised, so did the air-raid precaution citizens, and the housewives, who now became central to the campaign for survival.

For children, there was the requirement of the 'siren suit'. Maureen Owen of Sheffield remembers that:

> I was 3 when war broke out and I lived in a terraced house in Walkley … we had an Anderson shelter which we shared with the family next door. When the sirens went I remember being put into my siren suit and taken into the shelter.

This garment was really the first 'jump suit' – an item that could be worn over pyjamas, put on quickly and with the use of zips. Churchill himself used to own one, known as a 'romper', and this is on display in the Churchill Museum and Cabinet War Rooms.

There was a funny side to this, however, as there usually is when people are under duress and pull together. Barry Rawden, born in 1937, and living in Acton near the old Oak Common Railway Engine sheds where his father worked, has vivid memories of shelter life. His first story is of an unwelcome guest in a communal concrete shelter where his parents and a group of neighbours were gathered:

> … in came a drunken sailor and promptly laid down and went to sleep. After a while the smells he was making were so bad that we all crowded round the entrance of the shelter for fresh air. To hell with the German bombs, shrapnel and flack, etc. It was better than being gassed by the sailor.

There was more unexpected comedy in Barry's experience, typical of many accidents and bizarre events under the bombers. The family were in their Anderson shelter when his father's friend joined them for a game of cribbage. Then farce took over:

> Just a few yards away an incendiary bomb dropped, and out we went into the garden to throw buckets of water over it. What dad's friend, George, didn't know was that there was also a bucket of soot nearby from a recently swept chimney. Well, George picked this up and threw it and what with all the water being thrown over the bomb and us, the mess can only be imagined …

The shelters had to become all things to all people: passing the time was a challenge. In Stepney, there was a reading of *A Christmas Carol*, read in instalments, leading up to the last chapter, suitably, on Christmas Eve. Neville Coates, a Friends Ambulance Unit volunteer, dressed as Santa and came in with presents. Conrad Veidt, the man who played the villain in *The Thief of Baghdad*, gave children presents of sweets and cash. Women from the Save the Children Fund and other charities would travel to shelters to help amuse the children.

As David Hicks wrote in *Down Your Way* magazine in 2009: 'Everyone sheltering could only sit, wait and flinch at every explosion. Every rumble of gunfire from an anti-aircraft battery brought a similar response. It crossed everyone's mind that night that this could always be their last.'

In towns across the land there were the other more ambitious communal shelters, such as in Stockport. The town is built on red sandstone – easy to cut into – and there over a kilometre of tunnel space was dug to accommodate 7,000 people. Francis Rawlinson remembers them and says that one group of people there made their own subterranean bunker.

Pat Bishop has described the Stockport shelter like this:

> ... they were like caves. They ran the whole length of the town. They had a massive entrance and they were made of rock. They were very well equipped with bunks three tiers high ... they had proper toilets, a first aid post, S.R. nurse on duty along with doctors. They also had a kitchen area with tea urns. Volunteers used to brew up for the masses of people who went there. You had to get in there before the air-raid siren sounded.

There was also much inventiveness in places and structures adapted for use as shelters. One of the strangest ones was the use of icehouses: a feature written in 1980 by Arthur Osman notes, 'The icehouse went out of use before the turn of the nineteenth century and these deep and eerie caverns were either deliberately filled in or collapsed. In 1939 some had a temporary reprieve as air-raid shelters.' These were the deep chambers used in past times to store ice, with layers of straw between the ice blocks.

Also commandeered were some of the old police lock-ups. As an anonymous correspondent wrote to *The Times* in 1962 about these strange old circular isolated cells:

Always with us are the innumerable problems of what should be preserved in the interests of amenity, history or oddity and what should be demolished in the interests of improvement or progress ... the lock-up is one such place, several were used as air-raid shelters twenty years ago ...

He was right: they were very solid indeed and would have offered excellent protection.

Excitement and Challenge

For others, the first shelter experience was that of being uniformly conducted to safety street by street, as Fred Common recalls of the situation in Newcastle. He talks of the inhabitants of nearby streets being led to the culvert under the city. The city was bombed intensively; the New Bridge Street marshalling yard was hit and also, ironically, a German-built grain warehouse, as Sid Morton has recalled. The Wallsend area was a target, notably the Walker shipyards. The culvert is the Ouseburn one, going east through Jesmond to the Tyne; it lies beneath Newington Road and Warwick Street and covers the full length of the city. In 1907 a ferroconcrete arch was built and a solid floor added, so that made a fine shelter for large numbers of people. Not all underground tunnels and caves were seen as suitable. The Greenwich caverns were studied but not really thought of as appropriate.

For some, the first experience of a shelter actually in use was when they were at school. Norman Backhouse, for instance, was in Bradford, and his school had a brick and concrete shelter. He says:

The shelters had an open doorway with blast-proof brick screens inside the doorway. This made the unlit interior even darker. Whether these shelters would have protected us was never tested in Bradford, which suffered a number of raids, thankfully never near schools.

For Norman, the shelter was linked to some humour, and that was because of the gas masks:

We had frequent air-raid evacuation practices, when we assembled by class to go out to the shelters. We had our gas masks with us and sometimes had to wear the masks in the shelter for practice. By putting

Interior of an old shelter. (*Peter Langham*)

a finger in the side of the mask to pull the rubber off the face, a lovely farting noise could be evinced. We had competitions to see who could make the loudest fart until the teacher ordered us to behave ourselves!

Jean Foster of Sheffield also recalls the school shelters:

During school days we had to go into shelters and rehearse for about an hour a day in cold and damp conditions. They were long brick buildings. We were rewarded with two squares of chocolate afterwards. It interfered a lot during our lessons. Gas masks were important too. We all had gas masks cases, and if we forgot it we had to go all the way back home to collect it, which happened frequently.

There were false starts too, such as what happened to the family of Mrs J Blevin of Liverpool. Her grandson, Carl Mallett helped her to express this odd experience:

My family lived in Crosby and like most people, had an Anderson shelter in the garden. I was 9 years old when war started and was a 'sickly' child – got every illness going. The shelter was very cold and always had water under the duck-boards covering the earth floor, so was not a good place for me to spend the nights in. My father wrote to the Home Secretary and asked permission to dig up the shelter and put it indoors! This was granted and my father and grandfather dug it up and reassembled it in an alcove in the sitting room, to the astonishment of our neighbours and friends. For the remainder of the war we were able to sit out the raids in the comfort of our own indoor shelter!

Getting to grips with the Morrison shelter was something else. Children would all agree that it was a very good 'den' but this very simple yet sensible construction became a favourite – to mock as well as to use. Geoffrey Smith describes its actual domestic use very well:

It consisted of a very large steel table about 10 feet long … a steel sheet top with angle frame supported on 4x4-inch angle legs. A further frame about 6 inches above the floor carried square mesh floor panels to carry rugs or mattresses for the family to sleep on, and similar detachable panels were fitted all round to keep out debris.

In Norman Longmate's great survey of life in Britain during the war, he notes the sheer determination of Londoners not to let daily routine be disturbed. But on the Monday morning after the first large-scale bombing, one girl's story was typical of the chaos and the challenge:

The Tube was closed at Balham. I hitch-hiked a lift from a lorry driver who took me to Elephant and Castle and from there I walked to the City. We walked over Southwark Bridge as we were not allowed to cross London Bridge, and when I got to the office I understood why. Rubble and glass were all over the place. Firemen, who had been up all night, were standing round … They looked so tired …

The firemen were destined to be the heroes of the hour, facing gales of hot air as fire-storms developed in enclosed alleys and inside buildings. Along with people lined up in underground shelters, they and their hoses and hats have become iconic of that time and place.

The first communal shelters were in the basements. In John Lewis, for instance, customers could continue their shopping in the shelter: biscuits, books, knitting needles and wool were on sale down there. Norman Longmate neatly summarises the first ad hoc shelter facilities:

A Cheshire Red Cross worker slept in the former wine cellar of their house. A Sheffield family used an old, upturned boiler as an emergency exit from their cellar. An Essex woman still admires the reinforced concrete shelter built by her uncle in Hull, complete with double doors...

A cheap pamphlet on sale everywhere, even at the post office, gave the essential information for protection:

When a high explosive bomb falls and explodes a number of things happen. Anything very close to the explosion is likely to be destroyed and any house which suffers a direct hit is almost sure to collapse. Other dangers of a less spectacular kind can cause far more casualties. Blasts can shatter unprotected windows... There are three ways with which you can provide your house with shelter. First you can buy a ready-made shelter to bury and erect in the garden. Secondly, you can have a shelter of brick or concrete built into or attached to the house. Thirdly you can improve the natural protection given by your house, by forming a refuge room.

This is a workable mixture of terror and practicality. It was sure to send people out to buy protection and to seek advice.

Chapter 3

Bombings Across the Land I

'*Highly civilized human beings are flying overhead, trying to kill me... Most of them, I have no doubt, are kindly, law-abiding men who would never dream of committing murder in private life...*'
George Orwell

The Blitz, as has often been remarked, was a myth before it was a fact: it seemed to have a back story even before the first bombs were dropped. It made heroes as well as villains, but above all else it generated epic tales. The writers, journalists and artists had plenty of copy, and the shelters demanded attention, because they were the places where the spirit of community and resistance, optimism and humour, were most visible. Nevertheless, some writers pointed to the more unpleasant side of the matter. Tom Harrisson, writing in *The New Statesman* in 1940, said:

> When you get over the shock of seeing so many sprawling people, you are overcome with the smell of humanity and dirt. Dirt abounds everywhere. The floors are never swept and are filthy. People are sleeping on piles of rubbish...

But such over-sensitive responses were hardly of any value in a nation that was facing destruction – and London was not the only place to feel the might of Nazi Germany. A more acceptable and meaningful response than Harrisson's was expressed by Churchill's words: 'I can see the spirit of an unquenchable people.' Still, it was hard to ignore the fact that since the underground had become home to thousands of people, there would be problems unforeseen, such as a magistrate's comment in 1940 that for

A partially destroyed shelter at Bellamy's house and stables, Lincoln. (*Lincolnshire Archives Local Studies Collection*)

a young girl to go into a shelter on her own is 'simply asking for trouble'. There were undoubtedly unpleasant aspects of the Tube shelter culture, such as Kingsley Martin described, referring to an underground food store in London: 'Hundreds of poor people took shelter among crates of margarine which were used as screens for unofficial lavatories.'

These were moans and minor complaints. What was really about to grab the attention was the spread of the *Luftwaffe* bombings to other cities. Matters of protection and survival became more demanding of attention than comments on hygiene or bad habits of the poor.

On 14 November 1940, Coventry was the focus of the bombers. Then just after that there were over 300 bombs dropped on Birmingham. In 1941, British air strikes on Hanover began, in February; after that there were raids on Glasgow in March; Coventry was hit again on 8 April; between April and the end of May, Belfast, Liverpool and Plymouth were targets. Britain hit back with a raid on Berlin on 9 April when the State Opera House was hit.

London was still being battered of course. Chiefs of Staff reported that between 1 October and 8 November 1940 there had been seventy-three attacks on London. On 10 May there was a massive onslaught against London: there were around 1,400 deaths in that raid. There were only ninety-two ack-ack guns to defend London at the time of the first raid; those were soon increased and made more of a presence.

Gas

In virtually all the stories collected for this book, there are mentions of the gas mask, or respirator. For children it was naturally a horrific product of science fiction with its goggly eyes and inhuman shape.

The most notable feature of the provisions for defence was the awareness of the effects of gas. All the cities about to be hammered with the bombers had been well informed about gas attacks. As early as 1938 the Government had published detailed information about personal protection against gas. The very first ARP handbook was on that subject. Handbook number 5 was specifically about 'structural protection against bombs and gas in buildings; air-raid

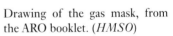

Drawing of the gas mask, from the ARO booklet. (*HMSO*)

shelters, either separate or in buildings. This handbook will be designed for use by architects, builders and others ...'

Of course, many men had experienced gas attacks, or had been told about them, in the trenches in the Great War. Thousands of people had died in agony at that time, and many were blinded or severely injured. By early 1937 civilian respirators were made, and 38 million had been distributed by 1938. There were many obstacles to the use of the gas masks: temperature rose in the mask, and so the make-up in use then was a problem, as were the hairstyles of the period. The mask would not fit tightly on a person with thick hair.

The first handbook spelled out the issue plainly and directly:

The use of poison gas in war is forbidden by the Geneva Gas Protocol of 1925, to which this country and all the most important countries of Western Europe are parties, and the Government would use every endeavour on an outbreak of war to secure an undertaking from the enemy not to use poison gas. Nevertheless, the risk of poison gas being used remains a possibility and cannot be disregarded.

The fact that gas was never used in the bombings did nothing to abate the profound fear of such an event. It all helped to instil apprehension in the civilian population, particularly when we recall that every man, woman and child was issued with a mask and had to have it with them all day and night.

The Great War had produced literature about gas attacks of course, and plenty of people had relatives who came back from the trenches suffering from nervous conditions brought on after mustard-gas campaigns by the enemy. Wilfred Owen, the poet and junior officer in that war, wrote of such an attack in his poem, *Dulce et Decorum Est*:

> '*Gas! Gas! Quick boys! – an ecstasy of fumbling*
> *Fitting the clumsy helmets just in time;*
> *But someone still was yelling out and stumbling …*'

The morning after a direct hit on a surface shelter in Lincoln. (*Lincolnshire Archives Local Studies Collection*)

The 29th of December 1940 will always be the iconic episode of the Blitz: the defining moment. This is because the City of London was severely pounded; it was forever etched in the national consciousness because the photographer Herbert Mason took the picture of St Paul's in the midst of the burning horror of the City. The cathedral, surrounded by flame and smoke, somehow survived – a symbolic event if ever there was one.

In the City at that time there were all kinds of ready-made sanctuaries, such as company basements and bank vaults. Ernie Pyle described the situation:

> Every block has a dozen signs of white paper, pasted on building walls, saying 'Shelter here during business hours' or 'Shelter here for fifty persons after 5 p.m.' ... I know buildings in London that go six storeys underground. When the banshee wails in London's West End you wouldn't have to run 50 yards in any direction to find a shelter.

Stories Everywhere

There is plenty of evidence that the atmosphere and communal sense in the London shelters was wonderfully alive and buoyant. One of the best records we have of that is from nurse Evelyn White, who said:

> There was great fellowship. The air-raid shelters in the hospital grounds filled with water ... so they converted the X-Ray department into a large air-raid shelter. They sandbagged it; they put in wooden pillars ... I can't ever remember laughing so much as I did in those days. I think perhaps it was a reaction, but it was great fun.

Memoirs of the London Blitz and the shelter life are not hard to find, but some give us a fuller picture, expressing a contextual view of the whole atmosphere, as in Mike Hollingdale's account from very early in his life:

> My family moved to Regent's Park Road, London NW1 during 1939. I was aged 3. Across the road from our newsagent's shop was Primrose Hill, close to the London Zoo and Regent's Park. Part of Primrose Hill was turned into allotments to help with the war effort. Also, a big air-raid shelter was built. During the Blitz of 1940 my mum and myself and elder sister spent many nights there, cold and damp. Also, just across from our shop was a brick-built shelter in Chamberlain Street.

Steps (hidden) down   **Boy standing on**
                             concrete roof

Two views of a surviving garden shelter. (*Joyce Edwards*)

This shelter was not very big so we only used it a few times. Around the corner at the top of Chalcot Square another fairly large shelter was built...

Mike then adds some details of other matters, notably the use of the Tube:

Although these stations were not official shelters, people felt very safe here. We would often go to Chalk Farm Station on the Northern Line. This was not a deep station but the platforms soon filled up each night... I remember walking home in the early morning, picking up shrapnel, still hot, from the night raids... At the top of Primrose Hill was a big Army camp that had big anti-aircraft guns that shook the house when they opened fire. We would watch the V1s, doodlebugs, coming in over London from this camp.

We owe a debt to those painstaking documentarists who logged events, and all kinds of paper records give us an insight into the experience of war and potential bombings. Even in the country areas, the evidence and the factual record are substantial. Derek Sprake, from the Isle of Wight (who we met earlier) has written about the school logbook from Chale, for instance, and the entries reflect many of the central issues of the civilian experience:

8 November 1939	Gas-mask drill and fire drill taken this afternoon.
14 May 1940	Air-raid shelter commenced.
24 May 1940	Air-raid shelter completed. History and geography lessons this week have been taken to give special lessons on France.
16 October 1940	Mr B Colton is absent from school today as he has been called for military service.
4 September 1941	Hot midday meal was provided for the children for the first time today. Miss J Russell, cook.
14 January 1944	Miss Loosemore fell off a desk this morning whilst taking down the blackout.

In fact, even as the bomber raids were beginning to be extended across the country to located prime targets, the experience of being under threat from the air *brought* extraordinary experiences to many, and the writers and poets made sure that they expressed such things. Beverley Nichols, for instance, writing in the *Daily Sketch* in August 1940, found himself in a country church after scrambling into a ditch. He set the scene with these words: 'The raid that afternoon had really been most tiresome. For one thing, we were caught in open country and there was no shelter but a ditch, which proved to be filled with brambles of peculiar virulence.' But eventually he and the officer with him found refuge in the church, and the result was one of those surprising but understandable side-effects of being bombed. But this day had been a happy one for his companion:

'The happiest in your life,' I had echoed, staring at him, for he had told me something of the rigours of his training.
'Yes,' he nodded, 'by far the happiest.'
And since, in days gone by, we had wandered through Italy together and climbed the loveliest slopes of the Austrian Tyrol, I knew that he must mean something pretty big...

Nichols' story was one of 'a screaming bomb, a broken journey, two disrupted lives', but that attack had been strangely moving and uplifting.

Even in the rural areas, people were busy with shelter construction and they improvised. On the Isle of Wight, Percy Sprake conveniently dug into the roadside bank where a stone wall existed through which the entrance was made…Substantial scrap metal supports were used instead of timber and the whole thing was apparently built to a high standard and fitted out with some spare furniture…

But generally, the provinces had known for some time that bombing was inevitable. Such actions as Percy's were, of course, very useful but some proper planning had to be done. In Hull, for instance, the Hull City Council met to consider the most sensible moves in the face of the possibility of fire-bombs and poison gas being dropped on their city. The Emergency Committee had a long list of intended measures, the main ones being these, recorded in Raymond Peat's chronicle of air-raid events for Hull:

- When a bomb fell someone would be required to find where the bomb had fallen and what help was needed
- People would be hurt so ambulances, first-aiders, doctors and nurses would have to be trained and places found to take the injured
- Fires would rage so men, women and also boys and girls would have to be trained in fire-fighting
- Homes would be bombed and the occupants made homeless would need accommodation.

The Committee applied logic and made a chain of precautions and actions for each plan, as in this:

Control Centres
Each area of the city has a control centre to organise the rescue services, fire and ambulance services etc., in their area. These centres to be housed in police stations, a school or specially built buildings. Men and women representing the emergency services sit around a table and listen to messages received from bomb incidents being read out…and they then decide how many ambulances etc. to send to the incident.

What did the Nazis primarily want to achieve? The idea was to destroy civilian morale. The bombing began with sheer blast effects, and then progressed to incendiary bombs. The attacks across Britain in 1940–1941 took around 42,000 lives and wounded thousands more than that figure, but morale was not destroyed. Instead of that, there was a sense of being together, of the unity of the people, regardless of who they were. As in the Great War, situations were created in which class was transcended. The writer, J B Priestley wrote in one of his broadcasts, 'Britain is being bombed, blasted and burned into democracy.'

The chronicle of bombings followed this pattern:

Phase One: September 1940 to May 1941. The London Blitz and other cities, mainly Coventry (November 1940).

Phase Two: Spring, 1942 – the Baedeker raids on Bath and the South, with 'tip and run' raids in a variety of locations.

Phase Three: Early 1944: a major attack on London, and the first flying bomb.

Phase Four: June to August 1944, over 8,000 flying bombs – 'doodlebugs' – launched and 5,000 of these were aimed at London and the South East.

Phase Five: Other flying bombs across the land, the very last one being in Hertfordshire on 29 March 1945.

E R Chamberlain has summarised the losses:

The maximum tonnage of high explosives dropped on any provincial city was 2,000; London received more than 12,000 tons. It was bombed continuously for a far greater period than any other city, being raided for seventy-six continuous nights … 60 per cent of all houses damaged or destroyed by enemy action were the homes of Londoners …

The consequences were not only dire for Britain: there was revenge of course, and the Allied bombing of Dresden and Hamburg surpassed the dreadful statistics of air-raid deaths in Britain by a large number. The sense of uncertainty was naturally overwhelming, yet people carried on, sensing that every person had a part to play and that each part made the whole more secure, and so success or survival was possible.

Important ports were top of the list for the *Luftwaffe*. Stories about time spent in shelters – official or home-made efforts – have been collected in my files after appeals in local newspapers for people's stories.

Southampton

Southampton was hit most severely on 23 and 30 November, and on 10 December, 1940. There were fifty-seven attacks in all as it was an important port and a top strategic target; there were over 30,000 incendiary bombs dropped and over 40,000 buildings were destroyed. The city's 'Blitz' refers mainly to these November and December raids: horror stories abound from those times. One bomb landed on the Arts Block in the Civic Centre and there were children inside. Twelve bombs hit the building directly and so 500lb of explosives hit their target. There was a shelter, but inside that, fourteen children died. One child came out alive.

Doris Lowdon recalls being out at the pictures on one night of the most severe bombing. She and her husband were caught out in the open. A bomb fell close, and after throwing themselves on the ground, a warden said they must get to a shelter. Doris wrote:

> Finally we got to the shelter and did not come out until the 'All clear' siren had sounded. It was morning before we came out of the shelter. We saw that the High Street shops were gutted, there was hardly anything left standing. But it didn't deter some of the people. Wardens were handing out big mugs of hot tea to warm us up from the shock of the night before, which some of us will never forget.

Plymouth

Along the coast, Plymouth had its main Blitz in March 1941. A group of Heinkel bombers arrived on the evening of 20 March, and others followed. In the early hours of 21 March the city was in flames. One of the most tragic stories here was that the maternity ward at the City Hospital was hit: nineteen children died there that night.

The damp Anderson shelters were used, along with all kinds of others. But there were also public underground air-raid shelters, and some were massive, being, as Steve Johnson has described, 'like a virtual underground village'. By the end of 1940, these underground shelters had been put into use and everyone in the area was close to that kind of cover. Steve writes: 'Stories of near misses and of those who had been "bombed out" would be passed around over a thermos of tea and a slice of bread and butter.'

In these underground shelters, there is art very much in evidence: satirical images of Hitler, Morse code utterances and varieties of whimsical graffiti from the time. There were two basic types of shelter: one using an arch structure and the other a square one. These were the shapings of the tunnel cross-sections. Steve Johnson notes that:

> Basically shelters worked on a damage limitation plan. If you were in the actual part of the shelter that took a direct hit…tough, but if you were just around the right-angle bend, then you would probably be alright.

The shelters had toilet compartments also; above they were covered with earth, and the square ones had strong support girders. There were also escape hatches in place, so if an entrance was hit and blocked, there was a vertical exit. Of course, at the time gas was considered a possibility, so there were ventilation grilles, and gas blinds were used at the point of entry.

Steve Johnson's collection at his cyber-heritage site also has something very rare: a ghost picture. As he writes of the time he took the picture: 'There was no smoke, mist or dust, wind, etc. that could explain this and nothing was seen visually in our torch beams at the time the photo was taken…'

There was a severe attack and horrendous damage done at Portland Square, and Miss Jeanette Hipsey recalls that sixty-two civilians were killed on that occasion. But in Plymouth, as Jeanette adds, the presence of the shelters was felt decades after the war. When she was working at the University of Plymouth (then a polytechnic) in the 1980s, the estates department decided to install a satellite dish. The low-loader arrived and the wheels disappeared down the entrance of an old air-raid shelter. It was under the old playground.

In Jeanette's case, she knew about shelters in Maidenhead, where she was born: she recalls being in a communal shelter in Woodlands Park, and also being in a shelter with her sister, one of them being in a cot. They had shelves full of apples from the garden around them.

Rich Avery has written that his grandfather built an underground Anderson shelter. He says:

All smiles in the Anderson. (*Rich Avery*)

Hard at work. (*Rich Avery*)

The shelter in shade. (*Rich Avery*)

A survivor outside the Anderson. (*Rich Avery*)

In late May 1943 my father was born. Newborn children and their mothers were advised not to use shelters during the first two weeks as they were more at risk to illness in these damp, dark conditions than to enemy bombs. During the third week, (14 June 1943) when they were permitted to leave the house they were encamped in the shelter when an enemy bomb decimated the house and killed twelve neighbours. Had the raid taken place a week earlier none of my family would have survived...

Pearl Griffiths recalled that her mother lived in a flat at West Hoe and that she used a shelter beneath the tennis courts.

One day she was told that if the shelter took a direct hit it would fill with water from the Sound and the people would drown. When next the air-raid siren sounded she did not go down and stayed under a table in her flat. The shelter was hit and the people drowned. I was called by the same name as a little girl who lost her life in the shelter that night – Pearl.

Raymond Didymus has vivid memories of life in Plymouth in those terrible times:

One lovely day I was playing outside with friends and we could see silver planes glinting in the sun. We thought they were ours but then

Raymond Didymus Has a Lucky Escape

One night at the height of the Blitz on Plymouth, when my mother and I and the other tenants were in the Anderson shelter, an incendiary bomb knocked down the door of the shelter and dropped inside. It was burning fiercely and not far from it was a container of paraffin used to power the lights in the shelter. We also had wooden bunks and other wooden furniture. We were all trapped inside the shelter. One lady was screaming and we were all shouting for help. Luckily for us, our landlady, who didn't come down to the shelter, preferring to keep watch on the house in case it caught fire, heard us shouting. There were sandbags outside the shelter and she was able to throw them down to smother the flames so we could get out.

the sirens started and we all scattered to our homes to get down the shelters. Because I was on my own in our shelter I took a spade down with me in case I had to dig my way out. That day Goshen Street and Station Road were bombed and about ten people were killed.

At the time he was living in a flat in a house in the middle of Garden Street in Devonport. Of course, he was near the primary target of the dockyard.

Liverpool

In Liverpool there were eighty raids between August 1940 and June 1942. The peak was the period of a full week of continuous bombing that took place in May 1941. The city was a primary target for the Nazis, as it was the centre of importation from America; night attacks were launched, and planes approached the Mersey from the Welsh coastline, and pilots would have seen the lights of Dublin to the west, and so been able to determine their location.

One of the worst hits was at Durning Road: there was a direct hit on the underground shelter there on 29 November. There were over thirty people in a shelter there, in the basement of the Edge Hill Training College; a parachute mine hit the place and boiling water from the mains streamed inside. One man remembers that his mother did not speak for six months after that horrible tragedy.

Neil Farrell, from Liverpool, gave an account of the gas masks he and his family had to have:

> We also had to take into the shelter our gas masks: these were issued to every one of the populace in case of gas attack, and a large one for my sister Wendy. She was the baby out of six children. She was put inside it and laced up, and could be viewed through a large, clear panel. It was fitted with a hand-operated pump to supply filtered air to breathe ... We had to take them everywhere we went ... Amongst other things we had in the shelter were candles/matches/and a torch, just in case the electricity went off. Also, a tin of biscuits and lemonade bottles filled with water.

Barrage balloons had been put in place, and most bombing was kept to positions above 5,000 feet, but not much else could be done.

Belfast

On 16 April 1941 it was the turn of Belfast. In 2001, a BBC programme dealing with the anniversary made the point that the city had only a few air-raid shelters and it was not really prepared for bombers. The onslaught came at the end of the Easter holiday and 200 planes left the German airfields, heading for the city which had been called the least defended in Britain.

Stories were collected for that anniversary from various people, including an air-raid warden who met some other wardens for a chat: 'I would say that within five minutes of meeting them, those young men and a young lady were dead.'

What was surely one of the most striking and significant stories from that Blitz was the one told by Bryce Miller, who told the BBC about being in a shelter where Catholics and Protestants took it in turns to sing their songs: 'but he said there was a deadly silence as the blasts got closer and after one wave the strains of *Nearer My God to Thee* could be heard coming from the entire crowd.'

The death toll was high: at the Falls Road baths the bodies of those who died were stored; thirteen fire brigades from across Northern Ireland rushed to Belfast to help. Nelly Bell told one of the most dramatic tales, recalled from the moment she was just married: 'There were quite a lot of people down to see us, but they scattered and when we came out there was no-one left – only the ones who couldn't run away.'

That raid lasted for five hours and the sequence of bombs was as usual, something now familiar to those who made it their business to observe: first flares, then the incendiaries and finally the high explosive bombs. In the absence of shelters, many people simply ran for any cover they could find.

An article written by Jonathan Bardon has this account of the situation with regard to shelters:

> By the beginning of 1941 there were only four public air-raid shelters made of sandbags round the City Hall, together with underground toilets at Shaftesbury Square and Donegal Square North. Belfast Corporation was so lacking in any real sense of urgency that vital pipe fittings for fire-fighting appliances and building materials for shelters were not available... the city had no fighter squadrons, no barrage balloons and only 2,000 civil defence volunteers had been trained.

One very useful refuge in these circumstances was the crypt of the Clonard Monastery on the Falls Road. Otherwise, as Bardon explains, the situation was that the city was totally vulnerable to the bombers' attack.

Coventry

Coventry was the main target in July and August and again in December 1940. It was then a major industrial city, with metalworking industries at the heart of production. There had also been munitions factories there since the end of the nineteenth century. A large number of the production companies were in the same areas as housing and so, in this time before any zoning regulations, there were compact targets.

In July and August 1940 there were small raids; then on 14 November, a force of over 500 German bombers went for the city. The raid's code name has become infamous in the history of the Second World War – *Moonlight Sonata*. Some of the aircraft had specially-made navigational aids, and high explosive bombs hit Coventry. In one night, over 4,000 houses were smashed; fires were widespread and water supplies were insufficient for the purpose of dealing with them. For five hours the raid continued – up to midnight. Even Coventry Cathedral was on fire.

In Coventry, the statistics of death and suffering reached over 600 dead and at least 1,000 injured. Such was the extent of destruction that a German word was coined by Goebbels, the Nazi propaganda chief: he used the word 'Coventriert' meaning 'Coventrated' as a way of explaining horrendous demolition. There were two more substantial raids: one in April 1941 saw 315 explosive bombs dropped, and in August 1942 the Stoke Heath area was hit hard. In total, the raids on Coventry killed 1,250 people. As Bill Hopper summed up: 'It was frightening to think we were so near annihilation.'

Hull

The Hull Blitz was long and almost constant. Reports referred to 'a North East town' and people would assume that it was Tyneside that was being spoken of. But Hull was pounded. Notably, some dates of serious air attacks were on 19 June 1940, and then several other severe raids between May 1941 and July 1943. A committee from the Council had sat long before the outbreak of war to consider preparations, but incredible tales of heroism have come from the people's memories of that terrible time.

Ron Atkinson described a distant view:

When on holiday in Scarborough as a child we were told that local residents climbed to the top of Oliver's Mount during the war at night to watch Hull burning. It could be seen easily, from 50 miles away. Apparently, anti-aircraft guns became red hot and couldn't be fired any more.

Shelter provisions had been well thought out but still people had the option of having a shelter routine or not. Ron's family 'used to hide under the tables in the Blue Heaven pub during air-raids because if they left, someone would minesweep the beer'.

Alan Dent remembers a special measure taken in his family:

The house at the corner of Eldorado Avenue and Scarborough Street had a brick air-raid shelter built in the garden at the side of the house where we would shelter with other people from the terrace. Prior to that being built we sheltered in the cupboard under the stairs, which was probably not a good idea because it contained the gas and electric meters.

They then acquired a Morrison shelter:

We were in this when the land mine dropped and because it was opposite the fireplace the soot was blown out of the chimney to cover us in the shelter. My grandparents lived next door to us … and I well remember one night after the air-raid sirens had sounded my auntie carrying me up the terrace to the outside air-raid shelter and pausing to point up at the night sky where I could see two very small silver aeroplanes silhouetted in the crossbeams of two searchlights.

The Council built free, small brick shelters with a reinforced concrete roof; after the war these were converted into workshops and storage areas, as Frank Evenden noted. Several people recalled that workers came from Grimsby to construct these. There was plenty of high drama around life in and near the Hull shelters. Kathleen Baker has spoken about the scene at which planes came down to machine-gun people leaving the Savoy Cinema in Holderness Road, as she was living at the time in Barnsley

A Morrison shelter in place. (*Author's collection*)

Street. She brought to mind the sight of men carrying children out of a shelter, under their coats, as a factory burned nearby. She saw a German plane coming down onto the school fields near Holderness Road. Kathleen was in the crowd leaving the Savoy when the plane came and opened fire. Brenda Cooper was there as well. She recalls hearing someone shout, 'Lay down' and she says, 'We just lay down... we heard bullets being fired.'

Colin Broadley was also at the Savoy that night. He lived in Rustenburg Street, and he recalled, 'I had been to the Savoy Cinema and was walking home down Morrill Street with my parents and elder brother when the attack by the German bomber took place... my mother threw me into a hedge.'

Hull was a city brimming over with drama, poignant human stories of suffering, courage and innovative endeavour. Norman Lyons has described a scene he witnessed in the very thick of all the horror:

On the night of 18 July 1941 East Hull was heavily attacked by German bombers, with the Newbridge Road area in particular being singled out. During the attack a lot of incendiary bombs dropped down the street, followed by a huge bomb which dropped less than 80 yards from us... Gordon and I suffered the indignity of being blown on our backs and covered in choking dust and rubble. The rest of the family were very shaken but otherwise safe in the brick shelter at the rear.

Colin Broadley has given a vivid description of what happened to so many – the loss of their home and a transit to somewhere else:

> I remember during the nightly air-raids being roused out of bed and quickly dashing across the road to the shelter at the rear of an already bombed house, listening to the bombs dropping ... one particular night our own house was hit. We had to move out to my aunt's who lived at Arram. Her house was next to Leconfield airfield. This meant we could watch the Spitfires taking off to chase the bombers away.

Later in the war, sitting in a shelter, he saw the doodlebugs 'skimming the rooftops'.

Shelters were fine, of course, unless there was a direct hit and that did happen. In Hull, Robert Matthews has a memory of such an event:

> During the night of 17/18 July 1941 the *Luftwaffe* carried out a raid on Hull and amongst people killed were my grandfather, John Robert Matthews, aged 47, my grandmother Doris Agnes Matthews, aged 44, and their youngest son, Colin, aged 6 months. They all resided at 16 Franklin Street and had taken shelter at the Franklin Street shelter ... it took a direct hit and they were all killed instantly ... Their daughter Doris, aged 16, was thrown from the shelter ... she survived and later married ...

Clifford Dalton slept in a shelter over a period of two years; it had four bunks, and kept the family safe. But at work, in Beverley Road, he recalls one of the worst attacks:

> We had a workshop at the corner of Wellington Lane, on the first floor. There was a parade of shops opposite. This bomb ruined the whole row ... and everything seemed to drop into our premises. There was a chunk of rock stuck in the roof of our workshop, around 6 feet by 3. We got props and braced it up. It was left for a month before anyone came to move it.

Trevor Jones Recalls the Arrival of a Shelter

According to my late mother, our Anderson shelter was delivered by lorry. The corrugated iron sheets were dropped into our garden, making a terrible noise, then erected and covered in a foot of concrete. Dad had to make his own blast wall of wooden planks in front of the door. I apparently spent many nights in an improvised cot in it. Not everyone in Hull got one because they were means-tested so our better-off neighbours on one side used to crowd into ours, while our neighbours on the other side had a brick one with a concrete flat roof, built in their garden...

The tales of stoicism and fortitude from Hull are well recorded. Brenda Cooper's story is typical:

I was in the shelter in 1943... the house was being bombed. Just a few yards away my parents died. I went to live with my aunts. I can remember coming out the next day, going through a pile of bricks. I was told to go to where my uncle had a big house... I ran down there, a cat under my arm, wearing pyjamas and a gabardine.

An Anderson shelter surviving in a garden today. (*Peter Langham*)

In Providence Road, Cheryl Rickles lost several relatives. She noted that it was a favourite trick of pilots, on their way home over the North Sea and with some bullets left, to go for people coming out of theatres and terrify them.

There were little moments of humour as when, as Eileen Dewhirst recalls, her mother, who had 'lovely feet' went into the shelter and then kept saying that her feet really hurt. The problem was discovered – she had her shoes on the wrong feet. Christine Dent also has a bizarre tale to tell of what happened when she came out of the shelter. Her grandfather was thankful that his house had not been hit, but went to feed his chickens:

> He was greeted with a scene of carnage … His used tins of paint which were stored on a shelf in the chicken run had bullet holes in them. The paint had run out onto the chickens, they looked as though they had spent the night playing paintball.

Being in a shelter could play havoc with the senses and could create uncanny and disturbing scenes, as in Penny Wright's tale of two sad deaths. Her father had been out on fire duty and then came into the shelter. After a while he heard a strange noise:

> He only got one leg out of the door when there was a vivid purple flash and the noise of debris being thrown about. The noise they had heard was the flapping of a parachute – both of the people who had been with my father were killed.

Of all the air-raid stories that have a sad end when suffering a direct hit, surely the story of Walter Levesley must be the definitive one. He told me that his family had an Anderson shelter, and next door, close to their shelter, was a brick one. The sirens went on 23 June 1943. Walter was 16, talking to his friend Jim Owens. His mother was in the shelter with his sister and she called him to go in and join them. He relates what happened next:

> I went into the shelter and stood between my mother and father. My sisters were on bunks at the side. I heard the plane, and the sound … it was more like a tear than a bang … Later, I woke up, lying under

Betty Levesley – Saved by the Warden

Betty Levesley was walking home on the half-day closing break from her week's work. The sirens had sounded but all was quiet. She saw a warden along her road – in Staveley Road – standing at a gate. As she approached, he grabbed her and dragged her into a hedge. A German plane was coming behind, aiming at gunning some positions nearby where troops were billeted. 'It came down…I was in the line of fire,' she recalls. 'There were potholes on the road where I had been walking, made by the bullets…'

rubble. Most of my skin had gone. I heard someone say that they had found someone and I was grabbed by the hair, then taken out. My mother and father had died, and my sisters, though severely hurt, had survived. One of my aunts came for me and I was eventually taken to her place. But I was very shocked and nervous. I was shaking all the time. They took me to the convalescent home in Ilkley. After a few weeks I came home…but there was no home to go to. Jim was dead, and so were his family. The bomb had a direct hit on both shelters…

A bombed-out shelter in Hull. (*Courtesy of Hull City Council*)

The remains of a communal shelter in Hull. (*Courtesy of Hull City Council*)

Like so many in the Blitz, Walter was without a family. He was not happy with his aunt's and the life there, so he found work on the tugs and signed on in the Merchant Navy. Trouble was always in his life: the tug he was on was sent to Normandy and was used to help make the coastal bridges.

Summing up the Hull experience, it has to be said that, as Bateman wrote, there were times when people felt 'total despair': 'Thoresby Street school was in one raid and when I saw the flames in the sky it is the only time I ever remember feeling total despair.'

One particular archive of oral history, based on the life and experiences of Raymond Peat, offers us one of the strongest, most affecting accounts of the Hull ordeal. He began as a messenger, with a bike, doing air-raid warden support. One of his documented stories concerns a group of first-aiders:

On the 11th of July 1941 they sat talking and listening to the guns and bombs falling when the telephone was heard ringing. Expecting to be sent out, the first two parties went into the small room called the Control Room because it had street maps pinned to the wall. Just as they entered that room a bomb fell on it. Only one who entered that room was dug out alive.

Raymond Peat, boy cyclist and warden in Hull.
(*Courtesy of Mr Peat*)

Raymond Peat, writing in 1979, produced a list which is surely representative of the whole horrendous air-raid experience:

My memories are of children in the Hull air-raids, and thoughts of what it must have been like to be a parent in wartime.

The boy running during a heavy raid to find out if his auntie was all right.

The bundle in my brother's arms – the remains of a child.

The girl saved because her burning, trapped father told where she was buried before he died.

The four children buried under a house and gas escaping. All four died despite one of the greatest rescue attempts of the air-raids.

The children who watched in silence as their relatives and neighbours were gathered together and helped until the street could be made safe and casualties removed.

The boy who died with his father, trying to stop a roof fire.

It opens up other lines of thought to see the shelters from other viewpoints. Such a one is offered by the diaries of Walter Ernest Cook,

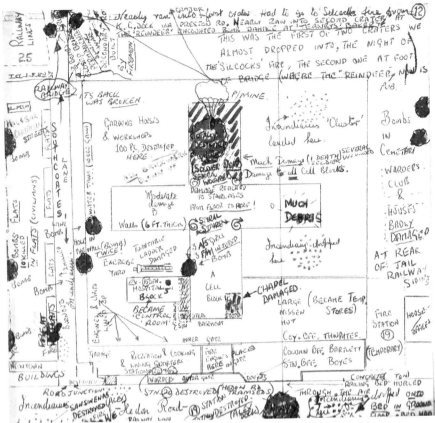

A plan of bombings and shelters in Hull. Made by fireman Walter Ernest Cook. (*Courtesy of Mr Brian Cook*)

who was a fireman in the Hull Blitz. In his diary he records a truly awful experience from the night of 15/16 April, 1941:

A long night of enemy air activity. B Shift off duty to report to 15 HQ Hedon Road … a solitary aircraft came in from the mouth of the river over King George and Alexandra Dock, past United Wallace Tank farm opposite jail entrance. I was outside of the brick shelter with six more people. The women and kids were inside. The shelters were crowded as the raid was prolonged. It was pitch dark and about 0300 hours a stick of incendiaries and a parachute mine were released … Incendiaries dropped … and exploded on the shelter (brick communal). From Newtown Buildings the whole area turned red … In the shelter were about sixty persons. Not one was saved. This was Ellis Terrace, Studley Street, opposite Holderness Road baths…

Walter commented also on his own situation:

Being in an air-raid shelter is reassuring but being outside with only a tin hat for protection is a different kettle of fish. The most dangerous job was the ride to incendiaries as usually high explosives would follow – or worse still parachute mines… any person who says they were not frightened is either barmy or a liar.

Glasgow
Every town and city had its own peculiarities, too, in their shelter provision. In Glasgow, in tenements, shelters were placed inside the square with the buildings all around them, along with the lines of washing and sheds. Pictures in the Glasgow City Archives clearly show the shelters, with their white roofs, solid and broad. One picture shows a

View showing external shelters along a street. (*Author's collection*)

woman pinning her washing on a line which is fixed to the shelter at one end. As the archivist comments:

> The shelters proved effective against flying debris, but were vulnerable to direct hits. In March 1941, a landmine exploded on a shelter in a backcourt off Dumbarton Road in Scotstoun. The explosion and subsequent fire devastated the shelter and surrounding buildings and resulted in sixty-six deaths and injuries to sixty others.

Was Glasgow too far north? That question was an important one in early 1941 on Clydeside. Would Hitler's bombers not come that far north? Of course they did. The docks were bombed most intensively on the nights of 13–15 March 1941. Eighty workers were killed at Yarrow's shipyard and there was a direct hit on the university. In the city, there was a shortage of shelters: 55,000 were made homeless. There were, as a consequence of the very high death rates when people were more vulnerable, not enough coffins. Juliet Gardiner, in her book, *Wartime Britain*, describes the situation:

> Their violent death in the Blitz was robbed of any dignity as bodies were trussed in sheets tied with string at neck and waist for mass burial, a practice the District Commissioner, Sir Stephen Bilsland, complained bitterly was 'indecorous'.

Sheffield

Sheffield was hit most severely on 12 and 15 December 1940. In total, over 660 people were killed and 40,000 were made homeless. On 12 December, there were three main groups of bombers and they arrived at Sheffield just before 8 p.m., dropping thousands of incendiaries. On 15 December, incendiaries were carried in place of high explosive bombs; Heinkels and Dorniers sent their bombs on steelworks, of course. As with Hull, there were many tales of courage.

Many, such as Maureen Owen, have memories of family members saying, 'That was a close one!' A distinctive feature in Sheffield was, as Mrs J Foster explains, knocked-through cellars:

> The other shelter was in the cellar of the house. It was in a row of terraces and each had a space knocked out into the other cellar walls so if a family were in danger, they could join others in their cellars.

Vincent McDonagh describes a typical scene:

> So many false alarms occurred that some of the neighbours left their own chairs in our cellar. The butcher from just around the corner would stand near the chute – and felt that he was an expert on aircraft sounds – telling us not to worry. However, in December … he was standing there and announced, 'It's all right. It's one of ours!' followed almost immediately by the whistling sound of descending bombs and enormous bangs shaking the whole house. A lady in the corner was knitting and without dropping a stitch, replied, 'It might be one of ours but they are still dropping bleeding bombs on us.'

The dire results of the intense Sheffield bombing have left us with some truly moving stories; Jean Gough has one of the saddest tales to tell:

> My dad was very upset … it was during an air-raid and his ambulance was full. There was a family bombed out and with superficial injuries. There was no room for them but dad promised to return asap and put them, he thought, into a safe refuge. Their house had already been bombed that evening so he thought they would be safe until his return. Sorry to say that lightning struck twice and they were all killed. Dad was upset for quite a time after that.

Mr Gordon Fiander has collected his own archive of drawings, plans and memories of shelter life and the Sheffield Blitz. His family were at 30 Flaxby Road and their cellar was connected to numbers 32 and 34. He also has a memory of tragedy:

> The parachute mine had a blast that shattered most windows and blew doors open, but it also dislodged fireplaces and Yorkshire cooking ranges away from the walls they were set in. The Hill family were the tragic victims of that terrible night. Gunner Hill was on embarkation leave: he and all his family perished.

On his birthday, 12 December, he recalls that he and his family went down into the cellar. He adds:

> Things got steadily worse as incendiary bombs were also falling, as well as heavy bombs and aerial mines. An aerial bomb exploded a couple of

streets away, blowing two streets in half and killing about twelve people. This mine was seen to drift over our house; had it hit us instead of drifting past, I would not be writing this…

Mr Fiander perhaps thought that his place was seen as safe:

A strange thing about that night was that as the raid progressed, quite a few people who lived up the street came to take refuge in our cellar, and at the height of the raid there were between twenty and twenty-five people in the cellar.

It is almost as if there was an uncanny sense that the Fianders' place was going to stand firm.

Other parts of Yorkshire were hit of course – Leeds had nine raids which took seventy-seven people and injured another 327 – but Sheffield was in the front line. David Hicks sums up the feeling of being in the shelters there:

Everyone sheltering could only sit, wait and flinch at every explosion. Every rumble of gunfire from the anti-aircraft batteries brought a similar response. It crossed everyone's mind that night that this could be their last. All the women were concerned about their husbands who were on duty during the raid. All were to return after that night, but it left an indelible mark on all of their minds.

After the years of terror in Sheffield, the Council produced a booklet with a number of reflections and factual data based on the city's Blitz experience. With regard to the shelters, this was the summary in the official statement:

It is generally agreed that the shelters of the City stood up well to the terrific onslaught. The comparatively small casualty list is evidence of this. In a few cases direct hits were made; in others, fire caused considerable damage, but on the whole it can safely be said that shelters were responsible for saving many thousands of lives.

The Anderson Shelter again enhanced its already good reputation. There are many instances where this type of shelter still stands undamaged amidst surrounding ruins.

The domestic surface shelter did yeoman service – those who have them may be confident that they afford the maximum possible protection.

Except where direct hits were registered – and it is realised that it is impossible to provide against this danger – all types of shelter protection did their work.

As a coda to these urban stories, we have to also remember that everyone was affected, even in the country and in the more pastoral and idyllic locations across the land. The smallest places had their incidents. In Skegness, as Jim Wright wrote, there were minor annoyances such as a government Loft Clearance Order which directed everyone to empty their attics, for, as Jim noted, 'Contents of attics would be particularly vulnerable to incendiaries.' Then, as men were digging trenches to make their shelters, a tragic event occurred – something that made the locals clamour for a delivery of Anderson shelters. Jim Wright explains:

> Then came that tragic incident in August 1940, with the loss of two innocent children. The Nazi plane involved was thought to be either a Dornier or a Heinkel, and it was little consolation that it was brought down soon afterwards by a Spitfire fighter over the North Sea... Somehow it seemed a cruel irony that a Pekinese dog was pulled from the rubble unscathed.

Apparently, although there was a plea for shelters, 'It was deemed that this was not a feasible option.' However, on 18 September, there was an emergency meeting in Skegness to gather funds for the emplacement of shelters, but Jim Wright explains the conclusion: 'At the same meeting came another, more resolute view – that any available money should be spent on munitions, "Not on crawling into the ground."'

Some of the memories of shelters involve little more than a trench. The novelist William Golding was serving in the Navy and in Portsmouth he experienced that kind of vulnerability, as his biographer, John Carey, wrote:

> He was there only a month, but that was enough to give him an idea of what the civilian population of the city had been suffering from air-raids. Portsmouth was the target for sixty-seven major raids...one of

them was the worst on any city apart from London in the whole of the Battle of Britain ... Golding told an interviewer years later that during an air-raid on the barracks, he had been alone in a slit trench with a thin concrete roof and a wooden seat on one side. There was a machine gun going off outside and he envied the gunners because they had something to do ... that night they went to sleep in their hammocks with a 500lb delayed-action bomb under a floor a few yards away ...

One of the most extraordinary pieces of writing to come from ordinary people at this time was a letter to *The Times* written by R D Blumenfeld – a man whose name would have made him subject to abuse and violence in some parts of the country. He wrote, after looking towards London and seeing the 'fireworks' of the bombing, about some local carol singers:

> These little carol singers, future men of England, walking mile after mile in the darkened country lanes, singing their age-old carols, unmindful of the portents above, are proof that, like the rest of the nation, they are the Spirit that knows no defeat.

This tone of poetic elegy for English virtues and home soil was to be a feature of the propaganda as well as of the natural outpouring of patriotic resilience which was to come.

Chapter 4

Health Matters

*'In the event of an epidemic, the procedure described in A above, will
be immediately discontinued, and face pieces will be disinfected ...'*
Air Raid Precaution Handbook No.1

Shelters are all very well, and of course they save lives, but they can
endanger health. People are crammed together in a small, damp
place for long hours. A sing-song and stories for the kids may
create happy memories, but as we saw in the story of the drunken and
very smelly sailor who stumbled into a shelter and cleared out the other
good citizens, they could be risky places when it came to a virus or to
sheer unpleasant human odours.

People in several areas searched out their own communal shelters,
using church crypts, railway arches or basements. In some of these the
illnesses became only too apparent – people coughing and suffering from
something called 'shelter throat' along with other maladies such as
scabies and even diphtheria. Of course, there would also be problems
with insects down there. Journalists began to report on these topics and
what began was what Alan Field has called the 'long-festering shelter
debate'. Tilbury was most noticed immediately because it was so huge:
14,000 people could fit into its loading bays. Soon, many became cave-
dwellers also, some going out to Chislehurst.

As well as visible physical signs of ill-health, there were the mental
issues. There had been fears before the war that there would be massive
casualty figures of people losing their reason and needing constant
professional care, but these did not prove to be a worry – at least not in
the obvious signs of distress. But because there was a stoical mentality,
trauma and anxiety were there, but were dangerously held back, so there
were numberless spin-off signs of stress and worry.

The Government gradually became aware of exactly what dangers lurked in the dark recesses of shelters. There was the usual British move made to sort out the incipient problems, and a national committee was formed to advise the Government on health and safety in shelters; the chairman was Lord Horder, and in early 1941 he undertook a tour of the provinces to see for himself what hazards were there for those escaping the Nazi bombers. He went to Manchester, Liverpool, Bristol, Birmingham and Coventry, and he was not happy. He was all for the idea of dispersal and the use of small domestic shelters rather than for large public shelters, and *The Times* reported on his criticisms:

> Lord Horder … visited Coventry and Birmingham … and made a statement yesterday in which he criticised the construction of the shelters at Coventry. He said that after the first slight air-raid there was a hurried rush to erect surface brick shelters. They were put up so hurriedly that the erection of the shelters was so poor that they were now falling down. The bricks were flaking and a penknife could be put through both the mortar and bricks …

Horder even quibbled at the apparent cost-cutting done by the Treasury and was generally severely taking to task the measures taken up to that point. In February 1941 the authorities were genuinely concerned about the spread of infection in the shelters. Horder was the doctor to the king, George VI, so he was likely to be taken seriously. He no doubt had strong words with the Chief Medical Officer at the Ministry of Health, Sir William Jameson, and soon germ masks were made available.

Half a million germ masks were produced for public shelters; they were pieces of inflammable film, 5 inches square, with a piece of elastic attached to fix them across the bridge of the nose. They could be bought at the local chemist's shop for twopence. Someone also designed a more up-market one, described as being 'approaching in style the yashmak worn by Moslem women'. Sir William Jameson told the press that while there was no need for them to be worn generally, people ought to see that 'they were useful things to wear in certain circumstances'.

Medical statistics were published to show that for some diseases, there had been a marked increase in reported cases between 21 December 1940 and 18 January 1941. Pneumonia cases had increased from 906 to 1,548 in that month, and measles had also increased marginally, from 14,773 to

14,798 cases. Whooping cough showed a large increase, disturbingly rising from 2,355 to 3,251 cases in that period.

There had been measures taken earlier: by October 1940 there had been chemical toilets installed in most London shelters, but the problem was that these tended to be spilled, and of course the results were nauseous and unsavoury in enclosed spaces. In the large London shelters there was no way that a person could have a wash, either. It was high time that something was done to show how shelters could be both roomy and more healthy: a disused line at Aldwych was prepared with bunks and better toilets. There were even books donated and film shows put on.

The Horder Committee reported at the end of February 1941, and they recommended the use of sodium hypochlorite in shelters; the reason given was that 'it has intrinsic merit, ease of procurability and cheapness in bulk'. The compound had been around since 1785, when it was invented in France, and it was used to bleach cotton. Exposure to the substance could cause sore throats and redness in the eyes or sensitive skin, so it has to be handled thoughtfully. It can remove stains at room temperature. But in 1941, when it was to be used widely, one advantage was that it can be stored and transported easily and safely.

A company called Milton Proprietary did very well with the disinfectant. At their seventeenth general meeting in February 1941 they recorded a profit of £24,430 before tax. In their report they very proudly said:

In August last a medical official of the largest water undertaking in the country broadcasting a talk on the sterilisation of water in war emergencies recommended the use of hypochlorite antiseptics and mentioned Milton by name. We welcomed this authoritative endorsement of the value of Milton for the purpose, which has long been recognised in tropical countries where this problem is not a new one. Milton is now being used by a number of local authorities both generally and in their hospitals for emergency water sterilisation.

By early March, Lord Horder was on the rampage again, giving talks wherever he could, scaring the populace and prodding the Government to do more for health in shelters and elsewhere. Speaking to the members of the Royal Empire Society he called his talk: 'Air-Raid Shelters: A New War Problem.'

Horder pointed out that advantage was not being taken of the opportunity for medical supervision in large shelters. He talked about the paradox of people discovering the pleasures of communal life in such nasty places: '...boxing them up where there was no sun or air, and where it had been an awful struggle to get a primitive form of sanitation established.' He said that it was 'fifty-fifty' whether people were safer in their homes or in the shelters.

Looking back in 1953, the media were keen to point out that the civilian population had been kept in good health in most cases. Sir Arthur MacNalty published *Civilian Health and Medical Services* in that year, reporting on the measures taken for public health from 1938 onwards. The book summed up the shelter health concerns with a theory:

> In seeking out an explanation of the lack of serious disease in spite of the use of air-raid shelters, the Ministry of Health find grounds for believing that some degree of natural immunity existed which was due partly to age and 'herd' composition and partly perhaps to the psychological attitude of the shelterer and to well-balanced rationing.

The Alderman Steps In
The good doctor was, naturally, very concerned about children in the shelters. Reporters summarised his worries:

> A big part of the shelter problem was whether children should be allowed to remain there all around the clock. There were children in some underground shelters in the provinces who had not been into the sun and air for three or four weeks. He had seen worse things during his tour of the provinces than he had seen in London recently.

With regard to conditions in London, in March 1941, the London Regional Commissioner for Shelters, Alderman Charles Key, spoke at a press conference. His statistics were reflective of immense production and emplacements efforts. There had been thirty-six new basement shelters made during February, and he noted that basement shelters then, in total, had a capacity to take 100,000 people. The capacity of every type of public shelter in the area then was 1,280,750 for day use and 1,307,250 for night use. Between the end of January and mid-March, 23,375 Anderson shelters had been made.

Key then talked about the first Morrison shelters being planned. London had been allocated 7,500 a week. But the sanitation issues were very much in his mind, in public shelters: domestic ones would be a secondary consideration for a while. By that time, it was clear that Tubes, basement public shelters and other official large shelters needed more supervision and more facilities. Local authorities were asked to supply canteen equipment for the feeding of people in shelters with more than 200 occupants. With very large shelters – those holding more than 500 people – medical aid posts had been put in place by early 1941.

The alderman was also an advocate of wardens being in place in public shelters: he created a system in which there would be one male and one female warden for the shelters with a capacity for 200, and three wardens (one female) for the very large shelters. They would be trained in the same way as the ARP people. Once again, England did what it specialised in: a committee was formed to bring together the various voluntary organisations which played support roles in the air-raid facilities. Print was generated and directions given, after due deliberation.

Children

At the time these discussions and provisions were going on, there was the question of how best to cope with the demands of the large numbers of children in the public shelters. The Save the Children Fund had plenty of workers for the cause: they set about providing toys and play centres to provide entertainment for children in the public shelters. A volunteer worker told the press that:

> There was thick smoke which penetrated into the shelters, so that we moved in a dense fog, but the children were splendid and the smaller ones slept all through it. Even among the older children there was no sign of panic.

Many of the memories from people who were children at the time are, of course, happy, in spite of everything. Austin Lawrence has written about schoolboys collecting cigarette packets and other items. He writes:

> United States Army soldiers were intercepted as they walked into Wenlock Barracks at the top of our street in Hull. We asked for empty cigarette packets...They were always friendly, had fantastic accents, and often left a cigarette in the pack...

In recent years there have been various projects, mostly involving oral history and archives, to document the experience of children in what must surely be called 'shelter culture'. Most children had memories similar to those of Ann Gurr, who recalled that her father dug the shelter:

> He dug out a long passageway and then a square room at the end of it which he then lined with wood … Next he made bunk beds for us, the room was heated and lit by paraffin lamps and I can still remember the awful smell they gave off. We slept in this shelter every night for the duration of the war … we tried one night sitting in deck chairs in the kitchen but the air-raids were so close we had to return to the shelter …

People planned in all sorts of ways for every eventuality. One person had a vivid memory of her mother always keeping a kettle full of clean water 'in case a bomb fell on a water main there would be water in the kettle for a cup of tea'.

Jim Wilcox has memories which must surely typify those of thousands of people:

> Hanging up damp blankets which we were told would ward off gas … Carrying a gas mask everywhere we went and using it once in a while when the police dropped tear gas to make sure that everyone carried a mask … Hunkering down under tables and beds during the Blitz, seeing flashes of AA guns and covering my ears from the noise.

Jim Casey from Bradford described life under the bombers:

> Our air-raid shelters had no doors so to blot out the light from the searchlights and the flashes from the guns and bombs, I hammered two 6-inch nails into the mortar between the bricks on the inside of the door and hung a blanket over the doorway …

Children had to grow up, as it were, to become little adults in many ways, coping with responsibilities and duties in the face of chaos and confusion.

Professionals were very concerned, naturally. Sydney Tippet wrote to the British Medical Journal in 1940 to put forward a very common view of things:

Children in Air-Raid Shelters

Sir, the medical profession will be wanting in its duty to the country if it fails to force the Government to take immediate steps to end the intolerable position of children spending their nights regularly in these air-raid shelters. It is extremely bad for the nation's future that this state should be allowed to go on. If the parents cannot, or will not, evacuate their children, then it is the obvious duty of the Government to do so. Accommodation must be found for these children in districts where there is little or no risk of air-raids. Children need proper sleep at night, not herded together, as in these underground shelters; and they must not be forced to spend all these hours below ground.

It is no doubt true that grown-up persons can stand this air-raid life better than children, but they too should be given facilities for sleeping away in safety at frequent, regular intervals...

Children also saw that shelters were not the ultimate, secured route to safety and survival. There are plenty of stories testifying to the horrors of loss and of the fear people had to live with. This tale from Hull is one of the most touching ones.

The great writer, George Bernard Shaw, wrote to the papers to express his opinions on the subject. As James Lees-Milne wrote about this: 'GBS wrote to suggest air-raid shelters for children. *The Times* refused to publish it because the editor was shocked by the implied suggestion that the enemy could, or would, bomb schoolchildren. The *News Chronicle* refused likewise.'

Of all the shelter stories involving children, the following has to be the most harrowing, yet it has had a very happy ending and the resonances of the truly horrendous deaths in the story told have a profound effect today.

A Reunion Story

Dennis Grout, of Hull, was 8 years old when Hull was bombed. He had an old picture of himself with a cousin, her mother and sister: for sixty-eight years he had not known her whereabouts. Then the TV programme, *Look North*, planned a commemorative feature on the Hull Blitz and Dennis contacted them and an appeal was televised. A response came from Mavis, the cousin. She had been living just 3 miles away. Of course, the reunion was filmed. Mavis had been adopted after the death of her mother and sister in the Blitz. The tale went on: her cousin Harry, now in America, heard of these events and made contact. A second, larger reunion followed, of course.

There are plenty of photographs in the archives of children clambering out of Anderson shelters, laughing at the fun of course, enjoying a break from routine. Most oral history records from people refer to the humour of wanting the local air-raid to go beyond midnight, so that they were then allowed to have the next day off school.

Memories are very sharp and visual, of course, and June Broadley's are typical of this:

> Another night I remember helping my brother deliver newspapers through an air-raid and at the end of the war walking late down Holderness Road to see all the shops and street lights switched on ... it was like Blackpool Illuminations after using torches to go out at night and putting the shutters up at the windows every night.

From the very beginning of the conflict, the papers had been packed with adverts about the importance of maintaining health. At first it was a matter of advising people to drink Horlicks and Bovril. Cartoon strips, line drawings, powerful texts, all combined to persuade the Home Front workers and housewives to sleep well and eat good food. Bovril was indeed the panacea. But as time wore on, the enemies to health came from elsewhere, and shelters were seen as a real source of danger in that respect.

Chapter 5

Bombings Across the Land II

'The entire town centre was destroyed and ... with "Swansea aflame" children were evacuated ...'

John Davies, *A History of Wales*

For the Nazis, 1941 meant a campaign against English ports and harbours. The description of the target was 'vital harbour installation'. On 1 and 2 January, Hitler's New Year gift to Cardiff was 100 bombers dropping 14,000 incendiaries on the docks and on the steelworks.

South Wales

One interviewee from Roath recalled:

> There were a few raids in Cardiff ... One of the worst was in January 1941 when a load of bombs hit the city. They were closer to the city centre but Oakfield Street and Crofts Street were badly hit and the Crofts pub was destroyed ...

Another person, who was 6 at the time, remembers the brick shelters. She had been out to the pictures and back at Queens Street she heard the sirens. She went into the shelter and sat on duck-boarding along the sides. She recalls that there were no domestic shelters: 'The raids were not over ... as soon as we got into the house, as we had no air-raid shelter, we all got under the stairs – including Laddie, my dog.'

The next month, it was the turn of Swansea. Over the nights of 19, 20 and 21 of February there were attacks, although there had been a bombing earlier – in June, 1940. On the 19th the raid lasted for five

HOME OFFICE
AIR RAID PRECAUTIONS DEPARTMENT

PAMPHLET on GARDEN TRENCHES

1. Where space is available as in a garden, a trench provides excellent protection except against direct hits. In order that the trench shall be clear of any chance of being buried under wreckage it should be at least 20 feet from a building.

2. The drawings show a complete trench of simple construction to accommodate six persons.

3. The bottom of the trench is 6 ft. below ground level and the width is 3' 6" at the bottom of the trench and 4' 6" at the top. It is divided into three sections.

(i)   A shelter, 10 ft. long, in which the occupants sit on a seat along one side.

(ii) A covered entrance, 3 ft. long, with a sloping gas curtain resting against a wooden frame.

(iii) An entrance, 3 ft. long, giving access to the shelter from the outside by means of a ladder. Over the entrance is a wooden cover or trap, as shown in figure 1, in order to exclude rain and gas laden air. The bottom of this entrance should be lower than the floor of the trench, to collect any water leaking into the trench.

4. The trench is lined to prevent the sides falling in.

The drawings show how this can be done using corrugated iron sheets held in place by wooden frames.

The frames consist of 4" × 2" uprights on each side of the trench, placed at 3 ft. intervals, with 4" × 2" spreaders fixed between them at the top and bottom to hold them apart (*see figure 2*). Instead of corrugated iron, wooden planking or sheets of any available and suitable material can be used for the lining.

5. The top of the trench, except the entrance, is covered with the earth which is obtained from the excavation. The earth is carried on a roof consisting of corrugated iron sheets laid on 3" × 2" wooden joists 2 ft. apart resting on 6" × 2" wall plates. Instead of corrugated iron, planking or other suitable material can be used. If joists smaller than 3" × 2" are available, they can be used, but would have to be closer together than 2 ft.

6. The gas curtain can be made of blanket. Light wood slats are fastened to the blanket about 2 ft. apart to keep it hanging flat and closely against the inclined frame. Twelve inches of blanket should be left trailing on the ground to prevent air passing underneath it. In actual use the blanket should be kept wet. When not in use the blanket should be rolled up the inclined frame and held at the top by cords.

7. The digging can be done in stages ; one of the advantages of a trench is that it will afford some protection at any stage of its construction (*see paragraph 14*).

In ordinary medium soil a single digger should be able to excavate from 60 to 80 cubic feet in four hours and his first step should be to dig the shelter chamber, 10 ft. long, to a depth of 3 ft. When this has been completed the six occupants will obtain protection from splinters and blast by sitting on the bottom of the trench.

Thereafter the trench can be dug and improved as opportunity offers. One man working alone should be able to do all the excavation in seven periods of 3 to 4 hours each.

The fitting of the lining of the sides will require at least two workers. When it has been completed, the wall plates, joists and corrugated iron for the roof should be fixed in position and finally the earth placed on the corrugated iron sheets, as shown in figures 1 and 2. The earth face over the entrance should rest against a wall of earth in sand bags, sacks or boxes as shown in figure 1.

At the two ends of the trench, the tops of the four uprights should be anchored back by means of wire lashings to the anchor posts driven into the ground, as shown in figures 1 and 3.

8. If the number of persons to be accommodated exceeds 6, an extra length of 1' 6" per person should be added to the 10 ft. length of the shelter, similarly if the number is less than 6, the length of the shelter can be reduced by 1' 6" for every person less than 6.

9. The length of the shelter shown in this design is the minimum required to accommodate 6 persons when sitting close together. With the gas curtain and trap closed, the air in the trench may become oppressive after some time, and it may be necessary to open the entrance and admit air, after the occupants have put on their respirators. If the trench is extended to provide a length of 2' 6" per person in the shelter, the six occupants should be able to remain therein, with the gas curtain and trap closed, for a period of 3 hours.

10. It is important to provide drains to prevent surface water from running into the trench.

11. If, when digging the trench, water is found before the depth of 6 ft. is reached, work should be stopped above the water level and the extra height required should be obtained by banking up earth above ground level.

12. In some loose soils it may be found that the sides begin to fall in before the full depth is reached, and in this case it will be necessary to use some of the revetting material as temporary supports to the sides whilst the full depth is being dug.

13. The design of the shelter is so simple that it should be possible for most persons to construct it themselves, and it may be practicable to use other materials which the householder may happen to possess. .

If new materials have to be bought, the average cost of the materials alone (excluding labour) would be about £8.

14. If circumstances do not allow of the trench being completed as shown in figures 1 to 3, it can be brought into use as a means of refuge from blast, splinters and weather, if dug to a depth of, say 4' 6". Walls could be built on the ground at the sides of the trench about fifteen inches high and corrugated iron sheets laid on the walls as shown in figure 4. A few inches of earth could be spread over the corrugated iron to keep the sheets in place.

The shelter thus made is, of course, not gas-proof and if, after a period, the sides show signs of falling in, some sort of lining will have to be provided.

From a pamphlet on Garden Trenches, Isle of Wight. (*Courtesy of Derek Sprake*, Men of Chale) hours. The King and Queen made a secret visit after the attack, and as one person remembers:

> The Queen enquired if anyone had been hurt or suffered damage to their home. Mrs Fisher told her how her house had taken a direct hit. It was suggested a memorial tablet should have been placed at this point where the King inspired the people of Swansea!

Ivor Lloyd has told one of the most terrible stories of the Home Front actions:

> I lived in Teilo Crescent and was 10 years old ... My parents left my sister and me in the Anderson shelter as they went to fight the fire that started two doors away. The doors to this house were locked and they had to break in ... There was no water from the mains so they filled the baths in other houses. The men then formed a chain to pass buckets ... a man had his arm blown off. My father tied it and told my mother to get him to a doctor ...

A dog is rescued – a scene from the Blitz. (The War Illustrated, *1940*)

One resident improvised her own indoor shelter:

> I remember my mother had a square dining table and matching chairs... When the siren sounded she would put the chairs on their sides on the outside of the table to form a barrier. She would pile all cushions around the inner edge of the table and put my sister and myself inside...

Others recall 'piling into the coal house' on a lower level from the house. 'We were standing on small coal... I had no shoes on,' says Yvonne Greco.

Joan Williams' mother told her that she had had to take shelter in a neighbour's Anderson shelter. Joan wrote: 'It smelled of earth and damp canvas; while they huddled together and the ladies made tea on a paraffin stove, she remembered the shaking and the explosions...' George Battye's house took a direct hit, but he and his family were safely placed in the cellar. His daughter, Deborah Tilley, wrote, 'Dad had vivid memories of being dug out from the basement and rescued by the firemen. I wonder whether his claustrophobia in later life was caused by this event.'

As part of this same BBC South Wales oral history project, Maureen Derrick noted that a cupboard had been their shelter:

> I remember one night in particular when my mother and I sat in a cupboard under the stairs of the house we rented, with her saying prayers over and over again and me wondering what it was all about and absolutely terrified.

In the January raids across the land, almost 1,000 people lost their lives and over 1,000 more were seriously injured.

Baedeker Raids

On 29 April 1942 the *Luftwaffe* raided York. There were eighty-seven deaths and hundreds of injuries. The railway station was destroyed and the Guildhall was also hit; the other main historically important casualty was the church of St Martin le Grand. But domestic targets were hit also – 9,500 houses were damaged. We might believe in divine protection, though, when it is noted that the famous Minster escaped unscathed. A memorial tablet now stands inside St Martin le Grand: 'Remembrance is hereby made of all those irrespective of church or denomination who were killed in York during the air-raid which destroyed this church.'

This was one of what became known as the Baedeker Raids, so called because of the famous guidebooks published by Baedeker (see below). These attacks were reprisals after the British bombing of the town of Lubeck. Between April and June in this year, several towns of historical and cultural importance were bombed.

The Baedeker Raids played a part in the later developments of British bombings on so-called 'soft' targets. The sequence of attacks and reprisals began on 28 March 1942 when RAF Bomber Command attacked Lubeck and, as has often been asked, why smash an attractive medieval port on the Baltic coast – a place with no real strategic importance? It happened after a scientist called Franz Lindemann was asked to study Hull and the effects of those bombings on the population. What emerged was a point about morale. Losing one's home certainly affected morale, and thousands in Hull were homeless. Lubeck was a tit-for-tat action in that sense. 'Bomber' Harris sorted out his German 'soft' target and 234 British planes dropped 300 tons of explosives and incendiaries on the place and killed 320 people.

Josef Goebbels, who kept a war diary, noted: 'The English air-raids have increased in scope and importance. If they can be continued for weeks on these lines, they might conceivably have a demoralising effect on the population.' Sure enough, Harris then set about raiding Rostock and Augsburg. Sir Archibald Sinclair, the Air Minister, told a group at a Savoy Hotel luncheon, 'Our air strength grows, and it grows fast... we will repay them!'

Hitler then started the reprisals, and the spirit of the campaign was summed up by Baron Gustav von Sturm: 'We shall go out and bomb every building in Britain marked with three stars in the Baedeker Guide.' They started with Bath, then Norwich, Exeter, York and others. In the five main targets of these raids – Exeter, Bath, Norwich, York and Canterbury – 1,637 civilians were killed. In contrast, British attacks on Hamburg and Dresden killed around 150,000 people. Hitler's fury had led to an unstoppable interchange of terror from the skies.

Even before these raids began, experts were giving thought to the possibilities of reconstructing lost treasures of our architectural heritage. The architect of Portmeirion, Clough Williams-Ellis, had this to say in January 1941 just as the first Baedeker Raids were happening, with regard to the Wren churches:

Apart from original Wren drafts, I believe that pretty well every one of his buildings has been accurately surveyed, measured and recorded in complete detail, so that, with photographs, far more exhaustive working drawings could probably be handed to a reconstructor than were ever given to the original builders...

Exeter

In a feature called *Living Here* Tony Lethbridge recalled his grandfather preparing for war:

> ...Bill decided to build a shelter in the playing fields at the bottom of his garden. This was a trench lined and covered with old carpets which afforded simple protection for the family and their neighbours. The old carpets had been given to Bill by a shopkeeper to whom he delivered stock. The carpets had evidently been in storage a long time as following the first alert those taking shelter had emerged very dusty and grubby... Prior to the trench being dug, Kathleen had insisted on taking shelter in the toilet which was situated under the stairs in the house. She was so frightened that she totally failed to realise the danger of sitting directly beneath a cast iron cistern!

Edmund Forte, compiling his family history, noted that 'Air-raid sirens dominated our lives. The war presented a variety of experiences during our formative years. Our daily lives were organised by the grown-ups...' Edmund clearly recalls the Morrison shelter:

> The Morrison was extremely effective, if assembled correctly, and undoubtedly saved many lives. My most enduring memory is of one of the nightly air-raids. Sirens going off in the blackout filled us all with fear... when the siren's first warning growls slowly rose to its howl, we knew it was a signal to quickly take cover... sometimes we were placed in special metal cages [the Morrison] which had been moved to the front room. Here we made our bed and snuggled up close together...

Edmund adds that 'We were all united in fear when we were being bombed, with the grown-ups pretending to be as brave as they could for our sakes.'

The city suffered quite severely, and desperate efforts were made to protect the heritage sites: a brick wall was built along the front of the Guildhall. But St Lawrence's church, a Saxon survival, was destroyed.

In Britain Now: Abolishing Traces of the Hun

DIVERS AT LOWESTOFT, Suffolk, search the dock-bed for unexploded German bombs and shells. One of the searchers is seen (left) coming up to report. So far a few shells have been located by these naval mine-clearing parties.

WATER-JETS AT PERRANPORTH, Cornwall, are used on the beaches to expose mines which, sown there during the War, lie deep below the sand: a converted Bren-carrier (above) hurling a powerful jet, its crew taking cover.

EXETER CATHEDRAL (left), damaged in the "Baedeker" raids of 1942, is the centre around which the city is to be rebuilt. Completed plans and models have been examined by the Minister for Town and Country Planning and await approval.

IN PARLIAMENT SQUARE, London, a bulldozer (above) assists in the clearance of air-raid shelters. It pushes the debris away after the shelters have been pounded to pieces by a heavy steel weight swung by a mobile crane. (See page 30).

PAGE 767

Images of some of the worst bombings, including Exeter cathedral. (*The War Illustrated, 1940*)

Cowes

Cowes in the Blitz will always be associated with the Polish warship, *Blyskawica* because that vessel put up a fight against the *Luftwaffe* during the attack. The main raid was on 4/5 May 1942. By that time, the RAF had its new radar, and that technology was very effective with coastline surveillance; in addition, Hitler had turned his attention towards Russia, so for various reasons, by the time of these raids, Britain was more prepared and a little more sanguine about hopes of success – or at least, of survival.

The first attack came at around half past ten. The *Blyskawica* was there for a refit, and its guns were in action against the bombers for hours. Cecil Wright recalled the night:

> The surface air-raid shelter which served our town and neighbourhood was situated in our garden but in spite of this we had not made use of it before the night of the attack. On this occasion my father went outside as usual but quickly came back into the house and ushered us into the shelter. I was 16 years old and had spent the evening in the Royalty cinema … My father and I were the only adult males in our part of the shelter and we sat facing each other in the doorway.

After the lull there was a repeat performance; as Cecil noted, 'Although the houses in Alfred Street were still standing it was obvious that not one of them was habitable …'

Colchester Castle

Even before the war, Colchester Castle Museum was working to be ready for any bombing that Hitler might bring to the town. Eric Rudsdale was curator's assistant at the Museum: he was 29 when war broke out, and he remembers the Air Raid Precaution officers coming to the castle; Eric kept a journal and this was his comment:

> The only way in which we are compelled to acknowledge the existence of the war so far is the use of our vaults for air-raid shelters. I opposed the use of Ancient Monuments for war purposes at the very start, but now I am compelled to admit that we certainly have the best and perhaps the safest shelter in town. Also, what extra fittings that have been provided – seats, lavatory, etc., do not in any way interfere with the structure, and in fact do not even stop the usual conducted tours of the place …

The Castle offered very substantial protection: the shelter there could house 150 people, and although it was very uncomfortable as a place for a night's sleep, it was opened twice after sirens sounded, and did the job well.

Colchester heard the sirens over 1,000 times: one of the main raids was in August 1942, when thirty-eight people died. A bomb was dropped on Severalls Hospital. In the Chapell Street raid eight died when over 200 bombs fell on South Street and Essex Street. The issue then was the fact that the siren for warning did not sound – people only heard the whine of that when bombs had already fallen. Later, in February 1944, incendiary bombs were dropped on the St Botolphs area, causing extensive damage to buildings.

Norwich

On 27 April 1942 the bombers came to peaceful Norwich, intending to destroy it. Parachute flares lit up the area and then came the noise of the bombs. Incendiaries were used as well; more than 50 tons of bombs had been dropped before the all-clear siren went in the early hours of the next day. The planes came back soon after and the ordeal was repeated. Ralph Mottram, a local writer, sums up the situation: 'The light of flames flickering through jagged gaps in familiar walls, and reflected in pools of water, the crunch of broken glass and plaster beneath wheels and feet, the roar of the conflagration and the shouted orders...'

Writer Joan Banger quoted one memory:

It was five o'clock on a warm summer afternoon and from high in the sky the dull throb of aircraft could be heard. No air-raid siren had been sounded. There was no cause for alarm. The employees of Barnard's factory at Mousehold saw two aircraft approaching from the south-east. As they made out the black markings in the shape of crosses on the wings they flung themselves to the ground. The explosions that followed were curiously light, sharp cracks, and certainly not the heavy and prolonged reverberations everybody had been expecting...

Shelters were made beneath parks, and brick ones made in the Castle gardens. As with all 'Baedeker' targets, there was a prominent historically important landmark – the Castle – and this made sighting easy.

A Horror Story from North Shields

Some events in the shelter story stand out as totally staggeringly horrible. This is one of them.

In early May 1941, Wilkinson's lemonade factory in North Shields was the victim of a direct hit from a bomber. Beneath the factory was a large basement air-raid shelter which could hold 210 people. The shelter had three rooms, and entry was through an entrance from King Street. Along the walls there were two-bed high rows of bunks. The floors were concrete but the ceiling was not reinforced, and there was a rear exit leading to George Street. The *Shields Evening News* for 5 May has the horrendous details of what happened:

> There were several killed and many injured at a North-East coast town early yesterday when a high-explosive bomb scored a direct hit on premises under which there was a communal shelter. Several families were wiped out and many others suffered by the deaths of one or more members. Children were included among the killed and injured. This shelter was extremely popular among residents of a working-class district on account of the fact that it had been heavily reinforced...

One of the more dramatic incidents was of a man pinned down by a steel girder. Rescue workers could not free him, and eventually the doctor said that his life could only be saved by amputating his foot. But in one last gargantuan effort, workers lifted the girder and the foot was saved. Many rescuers risked their lives with acts of heroism that night.

The Wilkinson story is proof that shelters were not a surety of salvation when the worst bombing came along.

It was well known that the girls in the shelter always enjoyed a good sing-song. The reporter for the local paper did not miss the telling detail: 'Labels used by the firm on their bottles were scattered about the street and by the irony of fate showed luscious fruit and bore the words, "Cheer up".'

Looking back at all this now, the Baedeker Raids appear to be one of the most senseless and wasteful episodes of the war, and in addition to the loss of life, the nature of the attacks as petulant reprisals only serves to confirm our negative and condemnatory verdicts on the likes of Goebbels and Goering – the first being the Nazi 'spin doctor' and the second the head of the *Luftwaffe*.

Chapter 6

Information Overload

'*Now what I want is facts ... Facts alone are wanted in life.*'
Charles Dickens, *Hard Times*

Obviously, what most characterised the Blitz was the sound of bombs and the consequent fear instilled in the populace. But if we were to look for some other defining feature, it might arguably be information. No end of well meaning literature began to appear in 1938–1939, as various scientists, soldiers and amateurs got to work on gathering useful information. There was even a magazine called simply *Fact*. After all, this was one of the great ages of documentary: the 1930s had seen the rise of the documentary film and then the novel followed suit.

In John Lehman's paperback anthology, *The Penguin New Writing*, there were special sections for contemporary documentary and autobiography. The urge to convey facts and document experience therefore carried on through the war years. But before the outbreak of war, the main impulse was to give facts. As far as air-raids were concerned, the volume done for the Left Book Club by J B S Haldane, called *A.R.P.*, which came out in 1938, shows perfectly what kind of information was being disseminated. Haldane, like so many, had been in the Spanish Civil War and therefore had seen the effects of bombing from close up. In his book he makes this clear:

... behind many of the stone barricades in the Madrid streets there were breast-works of sandbags, so that if a bomb falls in the street behind a barricade, the sentry will not be hit by splinters if he crouches down ... Even a small ditch or hollow a foot deep is very much better than nothing when bombs are bursting in the open ...

Haldane's book gives an immense amount of information on shelters: he spells out the best kind of cellar for shelter purposes but speculates on various types of considerations, often ending at a dead end, even when considering basements: 'many of them give on yards at their own level. Others cover an area of thousands of square feet, and a bomb penetrating the basement at any point and then exploding would probably kill everyone in it.'

Haldane's thinking represents so much that was over-ambitious at the time. He included detailed plans of trench systems in his book, and had grand designs:

> It would be quite possible to build trenches in the London parks and public gardens which would hold the whole population, and if there were an open space within 100 yards of every house, as if for example the case in parks, then the trenches would be ideal there...

He explained the notion of a cellular cellar, and again used his Spanish knowledge to show the virtues of such places but adds that gaps must be built in: 'The shock must be prevented from travelling in a sharply defined wave by gaps of various kinds, filled with earth or air.'

His Majesty's Stationery Office was also busy producing lots of information. Eight handbooks appeared in 1938, covering the subjects of air-raid wardens, anti-gas training, rescue parties and debris clearance, the air-raid warning system and so on. The style was cold and precise, and when it dealt with terror-inspiring topics such as gas it caused a shudder in the reader:

> A bomb filled with tear gas will splash the ground in the same way as one filled with mustard gas. Evaporation of the liquid on the ground will produce a cloud of tear gas which will render a large area intolerable to persons who have no protection for their eyes. This vapour effect will continue for a number of days, or until the area is properly decontaminated.

Derek Sprake has preserved his own archive of official government information leaflets and booklets, and in his book, *Men of Chale*, he includes various of these. The source of much of this literature was from the Ministry of Information, and materials distributed included 'If the Invader Comes' and 'Lights Bring Bombs'. The busy MOI churned out every conceivable kind of advice on all subjects which were considered to be urgent, and writers were employed to use their creative skills on giving the information the required punch and power. Instructions about what to do if Germans appeared in the skies, about to drop, were daunting: 'When Holland and Belgium were invaded, the civilian population fled from their homes. They crowded on the roads, in cars, in carts, on bicycles and on feet, and so helped the enemy by preventing their own army from advancing…' What then, should the British do? In capital letters, the message was clear:

> IF THE GERMANS COME, BY PARACHUTE, AEROPLANE
> OR SHIP, YOU MUST REMAIN WHERE YOU ARE. THE
> ORDER IS TO STAY PUT.

Most universal and practical of all must have seemed the leaflet on making a garden trench shelter for six people. Derek Sprake explains:

> This involved initially digging a trench 2ft deep, 4ft wide and 10ft long (which the pamphlet stated would take one man four hours to dig), which would provide protection for six people lying down. Subsequent enlargement (presumably if you had survived) involved lowering the

Outline of the trench work seen today.
(*Courtesy of Jean Gough*)

trench to a depth of 4ft 6in. making it generally bigger, with wooden supports and a corrugated tin roof. Dug earth formed a bank on each side…A ladder at one end provided access and an entrance was protected by a gas curtain…

As the war progressed, the Ministry of Information continued the good work, commissioning artists, film-makers and writers to help with the campaign to follow the blackout, never talk carelessly and to eat well, along with hundreds of other subjects. By 1943 there were around 9 million women in Britain who were housewives. The MOI and the BBC radio made sure that these women were fully informed on the matters related to war, such as rationing, healthy eating and 'making do'. The MOI told them: 'Thoughtlessness, waste, a minor extravagance on your part may mean lives lost at sea, or a cargo of vitally-needed bombers sacrificed for one of food that should have been unnecessary…'

The other side of shelter life was, of course, the danger and the drama. At extreme moments, people knew that they relied on the firemen and wardens, the messengers on bikes and the doctors and nurses, along with the stalwart members of the WVS. We can learn a great deal about the drama and danger of shelters from the writings of people like Henry Green, a London fireman who became a notable novelist. In a piece written for *New Writing* in 1941 he described a rescue from a shelter:

> I had made a big noose and as this lay around his shoulders, with the lower part by his outspread hands, he could just move these a trifle to get them over the rope…I told them to take up the slack…He was drawn up without a sound or a movement from him…In the end they laid hold of his coat, they dragged him over the edge with their fingers. Then he was safe.

The rescue workers had a really tough job. In March 1941 a police station was hit and sliced in two, and in one hospital five nurses were buried. Two London shelters took direct hits in that month and a heavy bomb fell at the corner of a site and killed eleven people.

Information also means that private enterprise gets busy too. From 1938 companies started advertising aids for shelter life. The best scientific minds were applied to the creation of gadgets and implements of all kinds. Drydex of Manchester offered, for example, the Drydex Candelite – 'For the table or mantelpiece. Can be adjusted either to remain on for reading etc. or so that the lamp lights automatically when tilted.' To capitalise on the gas fears, Siebe Gorman Ltd., a firm which had been in existence since 1819, had everything needed for the paranoia about gas from the skies:

Makers of all classes of breathing apparatus and safety, protective and first-aid appliances. By far the oldest designers and manufacturers of respiratory apparatus in the world and the first to receive the Home Office Certification Mark on gas masks.

Britain had even gathered air-raid information from Germany in 1938. Geoffrey Lloyd, under-secretary at the Home Office, visited Berlin in January of that year to study German methods of gas mask production. *The Times* reported:

The degree of German preparedness is certainly impressive, and the German Government is satisfied that it is much farther advanced than in England. On the other hand, the information that Britain is now producing at Blackburn about 2,000,000 'people's gas masks' a month has been heard with something like astonishment here...

Mr Lloyd also saw some public shelters in Berlin, built under an old school, and four storeys high; the cement ceiling was reinforced with steel rails and the Germans insisted that the chamber was proof against gas, splinters and even the collapse of the building above. The report continued: 'Mr Lloyd and his companions dodged through chamber after chamber, now climbing up a wall to peer through a narrow emergency exit, now testing showers, water supplies, lights and ventilation pipes...' He was then taken to see shelters for municipal workers in the Juden Strasse Town Hall.

Information and commerce have always gone hand in hand of course, and in 1941 there was a marked increase in the advertisements in the papers for shelters and shelter facilities. Anything that might ease the ordeal of a long spell in a damp and cold shelter was something that might tempt the buyer. Comfort took centre stage of course. This is a typical one:

All-steel tubular shelter bunks for sale: three-tier diamond spring mattress, rust proof, hygienic, collapsible; 60s. per tier of three, special price for continuous runs; immediate application necessary, limited supply only.

Indoor shelters were on sale for around £12 with the attraction of 'no digging, no concrete' and specific equipment appeared also, such as the Redhill bomb scoop 'for dealing with incendiary bombs' at a cost of 2s 6d.

The commodities on sale were not only the large-scale materials and devices: they could be items for specific purposes, and again the adverts came fast and furious to inform people. Typical of this was the Chamberlin Weatherstrip. The advert explained: 'For the past forty-six years Chamberlin Weather Strips and Plasticalk have been used as a permanent installation to exclude 80 to 90 per cent of draught infiltration at all types of doors and windows.' The firm saw their opportunity for a new market when the thought of gas being dropped was in the public mind. They were certainly busy: 'There are experienced Chamberlin representatives in most parts of the country, and a postcard to the address given below will receive immediate attention…'

Paranoia and media-generated fear were wonderful selling aids. Chamberlin had taken their cue from a Government booklet which had these words: 'No serious amount of gas will come into a room unless there are draughts or currents of air to carry it in, so any cracks or openings must be sealed up somehow.'

People also needed to know who was organising matters generally. The papers were always pleased to run reports with headings such as 'Good News for Shelterers'. This gave the MOI a chance to say impressive things and to give the populace a sense that those in charge knew what they were doing. In January 1941, for instance, as the Baedeker Raids raged, readers were reassured that a new 'logical division' had been formed to deal exclusively with air-raid shelters. What happened was that the Ministry of Home Security and the Ministry of Health had been defined as separate departments. In addition, there were regional Commissioners. In effect, all this gave responsibility to one person who would 'check abuses and remedy evil conditions down below'.

The reassurance was expressed in such a way that the MOI writers must have been involved:

In the sphere of safety, criticism continues to comprise two main allegations. The first is that the decision not to build more deep shelters, other than spurs from the Tubes, is callous and mean. It is a sufficient reply that two successive Ministers have been forced to the conclusion that the provision of deep shelters on a large scale would be impracticable…

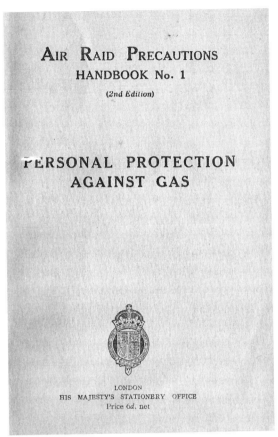

One of the booklets produced on gas attacks. (*HMSO*)

'Spin' was a fine art in war, as ever.

Information was everywhere, and wherever possible, it was in pictures as well as words. Even in the cigarette packets there was information. Churchman's cigarettes had a series in which such topics as protecting a window against blast or testing for gas contamination were explained in pictures. One picture even showed the use of a stirrup pump. Then, naturally, there were films. When people had a night out at the pictures, the main feature was preceded by a ten-minute *Pathe News* report. This was a focus on a chosen topic, related to the Home Front at times, and used as part of the propaganda machine of the Government.

His Majesty's Stationery Office and other publishers were very busy producing all varieties of information. A sample of the publications issued in 1938–1940 includes these:

Ministry of Home Security:	*Your Anderson Shelter this Winter*
Ministry of Home Security:	*Phosphorus and Other Bombs Now Used by the Enemy*
Lord Privy Seal's Office:	*Fire precautions in War Time – Public information leaflet*
Thomas Evelyn:	*ARP: A Concise, fully illustrated and Practical Guide for the Householder and Air Raid Warden*
Ministry of Home Security:	*Your Home as an Air Raid Shelter*
D S Merrick Winn and H F Hunt:	*First Aid in Air Raid Shelters*
Ministry of Home Security:	*How to Put Up Your Morrison Table Shelter*

In addition, as it was the age of documentary, writers were recruited to be involved in this channel of information. Poets and novelists were called in to add to the drive towards increasing morale and to showing the population in general that wherever they were, they were not alone. All the acquired skills and expertise in expressing facts and interpreting the world in realistic terms were applied to help stave off desperation and despair in the face of the bombing.

On the other hand, at local and regional level, information was well handled and its purposes more visible and valid. In Sheffield, for instance, as the city report after the war made clear, 'Early on the morning of the first raid, an Enquiry Bureau was established at the Central Library, where representatives of all bodies were present to answer enquiries and to give all possible help to the public.' This organisation dealt with such matters as missing persons, rationing, damaged property and billeting. One of its best actions was the creation of a searcher service to trace missing relatives. The report states that 'It dealt with upwards of 700 telegrams of enquiry. It spread information under rapidly changing conditions. It organised a fleet of loudspeaker vans to distribute information throughout the city.' There is no doubt that some of the forward planning of the year immediately before the war broke out was now put to good use. Britain had become proficient in delivering information to where it was needed. Arguably, most powerful of all was the campaign to stop the wrong information being spread around. The phrase 'The walls have ears' came into popular consciousness from all quarters and everyone knew that 'careless talk costs lives'.

Chapter 7

Enthusiasts and Nostalgia

'Nothing great was ever achieved without enthusiasm.'
Ralph Waldo Emerson

There is a fairly new hobby sweeping the nation: people are exploring all kinds of derelict and subterranean structures and natural spaces. The name for this is 'urbexing' – urban exploring. It is exciting, adventurous and on your own doorstep, as our towns are packed with alternative, unknown and often ancient places – locations of shadows, lost memories, past communities, lost technologies, and sometimes even ghosts. Naturally, air-raid shelters form a part of this abandoned wasteland of history.

There are underground chambers in thousands of places: typical of these is perhaps the space beneath the Braime factory in Leeds, which has two preserved air-raid shelters, or the Bridge Valley Road deep shelter in Bristol. They each have their appeal and their compelling historical interest, holding something of the people from the past within them, as is so often claimed in paranormal investigation.

This new interest is expanding on the internet, of course. A typical example of this is *Forlorn Britain*: here, the account of the exploration of the Bridge Valley Road shelter forms the focus:

Moving on, another doorway leads us to the first signs of the air-raid shelter ... in order to prepare the railway tunnel as a refuge from the bombing, the tunnel was lined in a corrugated iron structure to catch and divert the drips from the tunnel roof and keep the people sheltering below dry for the night ...

Note the sense of stepping into a dark, unknown world here: the appeal is clear. Urbexing takes us into a material world which is part of a massive and ongoing unwritten history – a story without a text.

Cyber-heritage
One of the most ambitious and fascinating examples of this, with air-raid shelters very much in mind, is Steve Johnson's 'cyber-heritage' site. This presents an extensive and detailed journey into the shelters beneath Plymouth. Steve explains the setting:

> In the long hot summer of 1939 Plymouthians witnessed the impending and eventual outbreak of World War II. The extended school summer holiday saw furious activity in the deserted school playgrounds, and verdant public parklands. Mechanical excavators were busy digging trenches in these playgrounds, in almost every city park and in many sports grounds...

Cyber-heritage is all about digging for an alternative past, untold and often uncelebrated. Steve Johnson explains all the varieties of Plymouth shelters and their construction, gathering as he does the myth, lore and social history of the inner chambers. In some ways this is similar to what some are now calling 'psychogeography' – the notion that in locations everywhere, layers of past time and people meet and conjoin, making a sense of history almost palpable. Steve describes what is arguably the main focus of this in the Plymouth caverns:

> So by the end of 1940 we can envisage a city whose school playgrounds and parklands are honeycombed with passages which during the air-raid conditions would fill with the jostling humanity of war-torn Plymouth, where songs would be sung ('Roll out the barrel,' 'Run, Rabbit, Run' and so on), where birthdays would be celebrated underground and where school lessons and tables would be repeated in 'troglodyte' classrooms...

By searching the West Devon records office in Plymouth, and by looking through the ARP sector plans, Steve located the labyrinths beneath the city. He concludes:

Ben Sansum outside his shelter. (*Ben Sansum*)

An alleged ghost photographed in the Plymouth caverns. (*Steve Johnson*)

A Ghost in the Shelter?

Steve Johnson writes about the picture:

'This is the ghost pic. Several photos were taken within one minute or so of each other; all used electronic flash as there was no available light, being pitch black. This image only recorded what appears to be two seated figures. The one on the right appears to be a torso with a bearded head, note facial details...the left figure seems to be seated and looking to the viewers' left ...the skull being seen side-on resembles an X-ray image. This site, although of 1940s construction, is cut into an area that was once occupied by a medieval friary. I say nothing, but merely present it to you...'

Just how many shelters were there and how many exist today? This is not an easy question. Records are at times vague, inaccurate and often misleading. Also, from the plans it is difficult sometimes to tell whether one shelter was built with six separate tunnels – or was it six shelters? Whichever way it is looked at, there were hundreds and probably 100 or so shelters survive today.

The appeal of nostalgia is as strong as the sheer intrigue of urbexing, of course. We need look no further for the profound affection for the 1940s and for shelters than the heritage industry and local or regional museums. On the former airfield of Hemswell, near Kirton Lindsey in Lincolnshire, now an antiques centre, visitors will find a café which recreates the ambience of the 1940s, and as one enters, the signs tells one that this is the 'entrance to the shelter'.

However, there are individual enthusiasts, and surely in a league of his own in this respect is Ben Sansum of Cambridgeshire. Ben has recreated a shelter, and also several period rooms. In a letter to me he explained:

I guess my interest began as a child, with my grandma telling me stories of her sheltering in the London Tube stations whilst my granddad drove ambulances above. Soon after, in 1987, John Boorman's film about wartime London, *Hope and Glory*, enthralled me as a 9-year-old boy, and my interest, particularly in Anderson shelters, really began.

Ben cosily inside his shelter enjoying tea. (*Ben Sansum*)

Ben adds that he more than celebrated the shelters, he made one: 'The icing on the cake for me was finding and constructing an Anderson shelter of my own. It in turn provided a unique setting to hold my 21st birthday party and is still a talking point of my friends!'

He then moved on to his next project – to own a house which was a home from the 1940s. Ben writes about his passion: 'Sitting down in the Anderson, two grown men in their early '30s, we're like a cross between two overgrown schoolboys in our den, and two old-age pensioners reminiscing about times we never actually knew yet feel so familiar with.'

Urbexing has several major organisations in its lists, but few can rival Subterranea Britannica. The society was formed in 1974 'devoted to the study and investigation of man-made and man-used underground places'. It has a particular interest in Cold War bunkers, but the remit is wide. Sub Brit arranges two conferences every year and publishes a magazine, *Subterranea*. As it proclaims on its website, Sub Brit 'is an

Four shelter signs from London streets. (*Courtesy of Jonathan Ginn*)

authoritative body within this specialist area of industrial archaeology and research'.

Jonathan Ginn noticed another feature of the cultural history of shelters – the signs indicating their position still surviving on brick walls around London. These took the form of a dark painted square with a massive letter S and an arrow pointing in the direction of the entrance. One sign survives today on a wall between two windows of a house, saying simply, 'D14 Shelter'. Occasionally, signs were made of metal as well. At 28 Queen Anne's Gate there is a blue plaque for Lord Haldane (1856–1928), telling us that he was a 'statesman, lawyer and philosopher' and that he lived there. Beneath the plaque there is clearly the outline of an air-raid sign. Again, signs were part of the underground shelter life in all kinds of ways. In Kent, shelters had signs indicating where the warden could be found.

Sometimes the search for the old shelters involves combing one's home town for the vestiges of the past which are still in the material present but covered over or transmuted into something else. Frank Dolman in Liverpool has done exactly that kind of detective work. He wrote to me with pictures and added, 'These are the best I could do – interior shots were not possible because the shelters were full of rubbish as you can imagine after all this time.' His pictures show a large brick building, now the Laurel Service Centre, and a yard with a metal fence surrounding it. One interior shot is indeed a rubbish dump, but the extent of the shelter space is easily visible.

Then there are the professionals: archaeologists are also interested in shelters, of course. Gabriel Moshenka has written about a project at Edgware Junior School which typifies this activity. He wrote:

In the summer of 2005 the edge of a concrete structure was uncovered on the playing field … The site was cordoned off and the school contacted archaeologists. Staff at the school had been aware for some time that air-raid shelters had been built there … but their precise location had been a mystery.

After war broke out, the school was closed for a while and classes were taught at home and in church halls; this was before proper facilities for school shelters were in place, and eventually Hendon Borough Council paid for shelters to be installed – at a cost of £258.17s 10d for each shelter. Gabriel Moshenka describes these: 'The records show that the shelters were fitted with electric lighting, wooden seating and chemical toilets. A year later [1940] heating, ventilation and better lights were installed so that teaching could continue in the shelters uninterrupted.'

When a geophysical survey was complete, Gabriel advertised in the local paper for people who had attended the school in wartime to contact him. Tessa Smith responded and her words were reported: 'She described rows of children packed so close that their knees were touching, suggesting that there may have been three rows of benches in the larger shelters rather than just one against each wall as we had assumed.'

The real delight in such excavations is in the human stories of course, and Mrs Smith had a good memory. She recalled: 'We chanted our tables, we did our spellings, we played hangman ... we took books to read and we sang patriotic songs, so we could have filled an hour reasonably cheerfully.'

There are enthusiasts at the school, as it is planned that the place will become a museum, but there was one other benefit and Gabriel explained in his article: 'Perhaps the best measure of our success is that despite seeing us slaving away covered in mud through rain, hail and snow, several children announced to us that they wanted to be archaeologists when they grew up.'

Of course, true enthusiasts can buy ex-shelters. At the top end of the price range there are the Kingsway tunnels below High Holborn: these were built in 1940 as deep shelters, and were used as a reserve war room, storing 400 tons of secret documents, and were also the telephone exchange in the Cold War which was the contact between the presidents of America and Russia. It was intended to house 8,000 people in the Blitz.

This place came up for sale in 1996 but no-one was interested. Nothing happened then, but in 2008 it was for sale again, and at £5 million. It has established a certain level of fame, as it featured in Griff Rhys Jones' television series, *The World's Greatest Cities*, and then was used by the Subterranea Britannica society for a special meeting. Out there somewhere there has to be someone with the passion of a Ben Sansum, someone who fulfils the criterion: 'We are looking for a purchaser with the imagination and stature to return the tunnels to productive use,' said Elaine Hewitt of British Telecom.

Any kind of underground space is a project for Subterranea Britannica. One of the most interesting air-raid shelter stories from their work concerns the Brunswick Tunnel near Harrogate. This is a survival from the York and North Midland railway, opened in 1839. During the Second World War an air-raid shelter was built inside the west portal, and there was nothing comparable for residents of Harrogate in terms of a large public shelter. The story is deeply ironical, because Harrogate was only bombed once, and only then by mistake. In effect the shelter was never used. But the images of the tunnel on the Subterranea Britannica site show how massive it is, and so its use if needed as a shelter would have been incredibly useful in saving lives. Looking at the east portal entrance today, the effect is eerie: two dark entrances lie beneath an old brick bridge. The whole is surrounded by foliage and graffiti has been daubed on the brickwork.

Putting together all this interest and activity concerned with shelters and the intriguing appeal of their structures and locations, it is entirely understandable that they are being rediscovered as places where the imagination may roam. They have a gothic feel; they are unnerving and they invite paranormal speculation. But more important is surely the fact that they are the most evocative creations of that time in which everyone was pressed and extended to steel themselves to an ordeal which had never been known before. Yes, there were people who could remember the Great War zeppelins, but this was different.

Urbexing and the revelation of underground life reveals not only a past layered with dust and grime: it opens up some kind of understanding of what the world was like under extreme duress from the forces of darkness and terror across the Channel. Younger people venturing into these spaces will learn by the exercise of the imagination, reading the past from a text of stone, wood, brick and cement rather than from paper and books. The excitement conveyed on the urbexing sites and the sheer delight expressed by Ben Sansum and others conveys exactly what forms this pleasure in the past. The reasons are matters led by the heart, not by the head. Maybe the urge to do this is based on the famous line by L P Hartley: 'The past is a foreign country – they do things differently there.' Whichever way we look at it, the new exploration of that alternative underground world will continue to interest and excite. Maybe a key text, which everyone interested will read again, will be H G Wells' novel, *The Time Machine*, which, written in the 1890s, considered the new underground world and projected it into the future, a sad dystopia in which the monstrous Morlocks from down below were cannibalistic and came up into the surface world to kill and eat the effete Eloi people. Such is the power of the subterranean imagination.

The subterranean life led to more than the famous 'deep shelter' mentality. Many in authority had feared, before war broke out, that masses of working-class people in deep shelters would provide a centre for disaffection and revolt. It was argued that revolution might be engendered down there. This was understandable, as with hindsight we can see that British society was still rocking and stunned from the shocks of the Great War, in which social class had been eroded to some extent. For some of the die-hards, shelters must have seemed like ideal places for rebel-rousers and socialists to make their Hyde Park Corner dotty speeches, and so corrupt the working man away from British ideals of class, social position and obedience.

There is no doubt that today the experience of life underground in that terrible war has attained the status of what many now would call 'iconic' – this is in the sense that the actual feel of being in that situation is something beyond the most strenuous efforts to be empathic. That is, how can someone today possibly feel that they can understand, emotionally, what it was like? Therefore, we tend to do the next best thing: to find and absorb the spaces occupied by those in that space of terror beneath the ground. It is no accident that horror films in the boom period of Hammer films and others used the underground as a scenario for dark, unnameable fears. One film, *Trog*, used the theme of a family of cannibalistic troglodytes living down the unused Tube.

The 1940s House

In 2001, the television feature programme, *The 1940s House* offered one of the most accessible and informative recreations of the place of the shelter in family life then. The blurb for the series is:

Imagine living without central heating, a telephone, a fridge. Imagine being in a darkened room, or being woken up and being forced to spend the night in a damp underground shelter. Imagine not being able to pop to the shop to buy a little of what you fancy ...

The programme was in the 'reality show' genre, and was set in 17 Braemar Gardens, West Wickham, Kent. The family had to do everything that 1940s people did, including building a shelter. Although the neighbours helped with the shelter, in a wider sense there was an interesting conclusion when the actors were asked about whether they felt isolated. They said that they did, and were not aware of any community spirit – the core of the stories from the time, of course. Michael Hymers, a true enthusiast for the period, and his family featured in it.

The famous writer and cook, Marguerite Patten, advised them on period topics, and on the air-raid context. What was perhaps most poignant and impressive was that the events featuring in the series ranged from the blackout to rations, and from gardening to listening to information about the liberation of the concentration camp at Dachau.

Blitz Street

The same concept was taken further in this programme, with a set built in early 2009 in a Cumbrian RAF base, created for Channel 4. The idea was to show viewers what it would be like to live with the expectancy of the German bombers on their way. The reconstructed street was suitably smashed by bombs exactly like the ones that were used in the 1940s: the SC50, which had 20kg of TNT in it; then the SC500 which was ten times the size of the SC50.

As Barbara Davies reported in the *Daily Mail* about the programme:

> During modern-day tests on Blitz Street, the SC500 caused a progressive collapse along the terrace, blowing bricks into the rooms, sucking glass outside into the street and sending lethal shards of shrapnel tearing into the terraces opposite. The first house is entirely destroyed. The last is intact, but its front wall is left bowed.

The bombs were to become even more powerful: the ones used against Coventry in November 1940 were the SC1000s along with the 1kg incendiaries. *Blitz Street* makes it entirely clear that the results of this were terrible. The concept of the programme was waiting to happen: there had been so many other attempts to show the horrendous effects of the bombing and of shelter life; ever since the epic documentary, *The World at War* in 1970, the media had tried to find ways of shocking the later generations into seeing and understanding the nature of the Blitz.

This programme is about as near as we can get to the documentary re-examination of the ordinary experience – the domestic front, as it might best be described.

In all these ways, the media have tried to create the verisimilitude so necessary to a proper understanding of that awful period when life was hanging by a thread and people needed each other in the town streets and suburbs as they had never done before. When it all began, older people wept, saying that they had not yet recovered from the 'first one with the Germans'. They were referring to the mental stress and the switch from a mindset of peace and rest and routine, back to one in which they had to be ready for anything.

At least the family air-raid shelter gave everyone a project, and a modicum of security, but the fact is that Hitler was making everyone live like a frightened rabbit, and that was hard to take. After all, Britain had beaten the Germans once, hadn't they?

Chapter 8

Life in the Shelters

'I remember the air-raid shelters very well – the smell of creosote and hessian…'

Patrick Child

People tend to adapt to the most demanding and bizarre circumstances. Extreme situations such as prison or hostage captivity tend to bring out special qualities in people, and that was the case in the dark, hidden lives of those in shelters. Of course, when the Morrison shelters managed to be spread around, more people began to use them and so stayed in their homes during raids. But there was still plenty of distrust of anything but a deep or communal shelter. Still, whatever the shelter, the point is that the population mostly looked on the bright side.

One of the most striking aspects of that transition from peace to war is that the traditional British love of home and garden, of family and stability, had to give way in many cases to a more communal nature. Although the 1930s had in many ways been a time when questions of community and neighbourhood were important in a range of discussions in town planning and in the media, basically there was still a central place for that affection for 'peace and quiet' that was ingrained in the culture. The thought of other nations bombing you from the air, an unseen enemy, brought a sense of belonging and interdependence. The old established notion of an outside foe bringing factions together worked to plan in 1939.

The bombings stayed on the front pages, of course. Sometimes they gave the press a major story, as in the death of the singer, Al Bowlly. Al, who was immensely popular, had only recently recorded a duet with

Jimmy Messene called 'When That Man is Dead and Gone' (a satire on Hitler), when he was killed on 17 April 1941. He had decided to stay in London and take the last train home rather than accept a lift, and a parachute mine exploded outside his flat later on that night. He had made over 1,000 recordings between 1927 and 1941.

But mostly the reports were about yet another direct hit or maybe a miraculous escape from ruins. People had to adapt and survive. They were helped by the media and the propaganda machine: songs, cartoons, radio broadcasts and local papers all played their part in the battle to maintain morale.

The more the war went on, the more the stresses and strains showed. Yet there were other considerations, along with the fear and the sheer forbearance required. The questions were often about how to fill the time underground or under cover. Publishers produced books of games and crossword collections specifically for that purpose; story times were held; lessons sometimes continued; people knitted and sewed as best they could. Boredom became as much an enemy as damp and foul smells. Going to an Anderson shelter was an ordeal really: the best way to alleviate the unpleasantness was to take food and drink, play games and tell stories. There were choices of course: a person could opt to stay where they were and risk it. As long as the blackout had been observed and all possible glints of light from windows had been expunged, nobody would bother you.

The authorities had to start regulating matters. Wherever there were gatherings of people, anarchy was possible and petty irritations were probable. The civil servants had to busy themselves with guidance, advice and orders. In Westminster, a notice was issued, beginning with a restrained, slightly stiff note:

By requiring this shelter to be open to the public during air-raids, the Westminster City Council has placed a heavy obligation on the occupiers, and it therefore appeals to the public to show its appreciation by protecting the property and interests of occupiers in every possible way.

The regulations were as follows:

SHELTER REGULATIONS

1. Instructions given by the shelter warden must be obeyed
2. Animals must not be brought into this shelter
3. Smoking is prohibited
4. Any interference with the premises and the goods and equipment therein is prohibited
5. Lighting must not be interfered with
6. Unnecessary movement must be avoided
7. On the 'All clear' signal being given, the public must leave the premises in a quiet and orderly manner
8. Litter must not be left

<u>**Breaches of these rules should be reported to the shelter warden**</u>

There were also other events which showed up some of the wider problems. One common tendency was for 'deep shelter mentality' to occur. The authorities began to see that people would often be happy to settle permanently in the Tube and other deep shelters, feeling totally safe there, of course. Attempts were made to limit the time spent deep down in that cocoon. At one point, Liverpool Street station became the focus of a confrontation that revealed this line of thought. A crowd massed outside that station as bombers came into view on a Sunday in 1940. The entrance was guarded by troops who forbade entry. But there was a long and noisy argument and eventually people were allowed in. Ed Glinert, in his chronicles of London, describes the scene:

> More people came to Liverpool Street, bringing with them bedding, flasks of tea, sandwiches, packs of cards, books and wirelesses. The police, ordered to move on anyone who looked as if they were about to bed down for the night in the station, were powerless.

George Orwell, in his diary, recorded the elements of shelter life in London at the time:

> Most of last night in public shelter, having been driven there by recurrent whistle and crash of bombs not very far away...Frightful

discomfort owing to overcrowding, though the place was well appointed, with element light and fans. People, mostly elderly working-class, grousing bitterly about the hardness of the seats and the longness of the night, but no defeatist talk ... People are now to be seen about dusk, queuing up at the door of the shelter with their bedding. Those who come in first grab the places on the floor.

The different locations for shelters, and their contrasting guests, also opened up a can of worms: social disparities became more apparent. One of the highlights of the events connected with this was the invasion of the Savoy Hotel by members of the East End Communist Party led by Phil Piratin. He was to say later, 'What was good enough for the Savoy Hotel parasites was reasonably good enough for Stepney workers and their families.' The police were called, but a confrontation was avoided when the all-clear siren sounded.

It is useful to recall at this point that many older people had known bombings over England before: the Great War zeppelins had visited England and given warning of what was possible. In the provinces, that type of raiding had been small scale, as in this report from a local paper:

It was comparatively early in the evening when the roar of a zeppelin was heard over the Humber, and also the unmistakeable vibration caused by the explosion of bombs. Soon our guns opened fire and the raider realised he was discovered. In the vicinity of Paull several bombs were dropped but all fell on open ground and the damage was nil.

People then had sometimes run from their houses, to hide in ditches and by haystacks, thinking those places safer than being indoors. But in London the zeppelin raids were more serious and city-dwellers knew the fear. Ex-soldiers also knew something about gas attacks too, so overall 'shelter culture' was something with an imaginative dimension yet not wholly alien.

However, in Hitler's war, shelter culture was going to be something else. The shelter was a necessity so the time had to be filled. With a Morrison shelter, of course, people were still in the house, merely lying under a string table. They would have been uncomfortable, but would have had necessities and a few luxuries to hand. The art of coping with boredom became the order of the day.

In Andersons and in public shelters the challenge of time-killing and keeping occupied was another matter. Today, we have to make an immense effort to try to imagine the life under concrete and turf that people had. As one man told me, at his house in rural Yorkshire not far from Hull, their shelter was a cellar. He said, 'It was just a big brick cellar, icy cold. We spent around four hours in there, freezing, and tried hard to think of things to pass the time.'

No Shelter but Mother was Sewing

Jean Sneath of Hinckley has written extensive memoirs of the wartime life. She describes the kind of thing that happened if there was no shelter:

We didn't have a shelter, nor could we go underneath the stairs as our pantry was too tiny. Our 'shelter' was the large, oak table in the living room. It was one and a half yards square with 4-inch-thick legs and most valuable of all, pieces at each end that could be extended, making our shelter 6 feet 6 inches long. Blankets and pillows were kept beneath it and my war-weary sister would try to get some sleep before returning

An old shelter entrance. (*Courtesy of Jean Gough*)

to her twelve-hour shifts plus Civil Defence. As the electricity regularly failed for varying periods and reasons, candles were left ready with matchboxes at hand ... The teapot and mugs stood ready for use but there was no food to spare ... a cloth had to be put over the cage of our canary or he would have sung all night! Mother would sit quietly sewing, mending or reading by the dim light ...

Heritage Plays a Part
We live in an age of reclamation. Just a few decades ago industrial archaeology was all the rage: projects led by enthusiasts no doubt inspired by Fred Dibnah and other machine-crazy hands-on historians made sure that we were all newly aware of the disused machines, vehicles and small industries around our localities. Now, in the twenty-first century, it is the turn of a more universal interest in 'people stories' and this has without doubt come along with the burgeoning of the computer age, when collections of stories may be quickly put in front of millions without them even having to leave home and go down to the nearest library or archive.

The full resources of modern heritage history are helping us with this effort, however. A typical example of this was an event organised at the new Hull History Centre by Libraries Connect manager, Isaac Acheampong. The Centre was opened in 2009, bringing together the University of Hull Archives and the former Local Studies collection at Hull City Library. Isaac created an evening on the theme of civilians and war, with the key quote that 'When elephants fight, the grass is ruined.' The evening, held in March 2010, consisted of audio and visual recordings by civilians, with contrasting voices from Hull and from Africa. Isaac said that his aim was to show the experience through the analogy that war and being bombed generally cause a 'fracture' across everyone involved.

Inevitably, these memories had tales of shelters. One man spoke of an area of the city known at the time as Bomb Alley, saying 'You heard the sirens and your heart dropped ...' Another person who was a child during the Blitz said, 'The teachers in the shelter had us singing so loud that we drowned out the sounds of guns and bombs ... or we thought we did!' In between a performance by a violinist, the audience heard accounts of a man recalling his father being killed, and another very plangent statement: 'Of course, after the bombs, there were the bodies laid out on the rubble: mother, son and daughter ...'

One local man remembered one night when he couldn't find his way to the shelter. Remarkably, he started walking into the country, towards Selby; about 30 miles away. He walked there and found somewhere to sleep, then walked back. When he finally turned up in the garden of his family house, his brother did not recognise him, saying, 'Mam, there's a kid here!' Refugees fearing the bombs and not trusting to shelters often walked with their families out into the country and just slept under a hedge. One family walked to a farm and the farmer asked them where they were sleeping that night. Their answer was 'a hedge' so the farmer found them a shed.

Some stories were horrific. One woman recalled an occasion when some children found a glove outside a shelter: it had a hand in it.

Through heritage work and with funding, the society of 2011 is learning about life in the wartime shelter. In Surrey, pupils at St. John's School have been given the shelter experience with the help of lottery funding. In the war, sitting there for hours with time to kill, the pupils at Redhill were fortunate in having their art teacher set them to work drawing murals of Robin Hood and other images from English history. Archaeologists in Surrey have recorded the murals and more work is being done on the physical environment of the shelter. The place will now be open to visits by children from other schools in the area. They will see pictures of a pirate, a man on a raft and a Viking long ship, all done to pass the time while the bombers were overhead.

At the Whithawk Primary School in East Brighton, people may pre-book and then experience a walk into 'The Trenches' – a school shelter. Steps with rails lead down from the pavement to the protected brick entrance, and then on entering, visitors pass rows of gas masks and bare benches, with a bell nearest the door, presumably used for the all-clear or simply to gain attention. Beryl Tucknot recalled her school shelter in the area, at Finsbury Road Junior School:

Our shelters were situated in the road at the kerbside. They were brick-built with corrugated iron roofs, resembling small Nissen huts. I don't know what protection they would have given us but at least we were out of the building. To gain fast access to these shelters a doorway was built in each classroom outside wall. The door was locked but the teacher had a key and would open the door when the siren sounded. There was a deep drop, rather like a dry moat, between the building and the outer wall, so a bridge was built across to another doorway built in the outer wall which led out onto the pavement and into the shelter, one for each classroom.

Beryl recalls making pom-poms using coloured wool and cardboard milk-bottle tops. These were used for decorating hats, cots, prams 'or even for the cat to play with'.

There have even been re-enactments: at Easington CE Primary School in 2007, children took part in a recreation of an air-raid attack and evacuation to shelters. The report on the event explained: 'We are asking everyone, including teachers, to dress in 1940s style and for the children to bring along gas masks they have made.' Adult volunteers played the parts of casualties, and there was even some fake blood and some bandages used. Lee White, of Durham County Council, told the press: 'This is a unique opportunity to show how archaeology and history re-enactment can fit into the primary school classroom, while at the same time highlighting the work the children are doing by engaging with hands-on World War II history.'

A similar project at Limpsfield Common in Surrey had found a new use for six shelters. A heritage grant has made this possible: five shelters will be used to encourage the roosting of bats, but one shelter will be an education resource to teach children about life in the Second World War. The archaeologists have also had much more work since air-raid shelters were rediscovered and written about. The benefit has been that the experts in digging and retrieving the buried past have been employed on this, in addition to the impassioned amateurs, and so a lot more has been done.

In October 2008, Stockport took its turn in the revival of interest in shelters – the town had had the vast underground caverns to use and that underground space has been made into a wonderful heritage site. Matt Davis reported in the local paper that there was 'A special event entitled "Standing Together: Remembering the Home Front" held in the shelters and Stockport Market to mark the opening of the network of tunnels on October 28 1939, which kept townsfolk safe during air-raids.' Though under extreme attack, the town had natural hiding places. Nature had saved a great deal of work in that respect. Since then, the tunnels have been open to visitors looking for the feel of the wartime experience.

As long ago as 1978, efforts were being made to recreate the dark days of the Blitz. The Battle of Britain Museum offered the public a look at several aspects of the RAF personnel at the time, and their everyday lives. This included their shelter:

> Almost every aircraft there has a fascinating background story ... The walls themselves served as air-raid shelters for the ground crews. These, too, have been reconstructed, but when the public walk through them they will find that they are full of small memorabilia of the battle.

That word 'but' in the previous sentence is surely indicative of something we don't mind at all – we want to see the memorabilia!

Memorials

Of course the Blitz also lives on in the collective memory. But time tends to erode the significance of events and also it may distort them. Although some might say that memorials are merely blocks of stone that we walk past every day, time has proved that to be short-sighted. Memorials do achieve something.

In Plymouth one of the worst shelter disasters of the war has been grandly commemorated. On the night of 22/23 April 1941 the north-east section of an underground shelter complex in Portland Square was hit. As Tony Rees, Senior Lecturer at the University of Plymouth explained in the unveiling event on 23 April 2009:

> By the end of 1939, in preparation for the expected aerial onslaught, many air-raid shelters of varying types and sizes had been built which would withstand all but a direct hit. One which was originally planned to cope with a capacity of 1,000 was constructed as an underground complex in the Victorian park of Portland Square. It was broadly in quarter sections (some interconnected) with the Air Raid Precaution Warden's hut sited above the south-east quarter.

It was a horrendous tragedy by any standards. John Cornelius was interviewed by the *Plymouth Herald* about this, as his mother and father both died in the raid. He was just 13 at the time, and was staying with his grandmother in Crapstone. John gave the paper a clear memory of the shelter: 'It was very dank, very tight, and there were wooden benches.

You went down some steep steps to get inside and turned left or right...It was lit by electric light I think.'

The only living survivor in 2009 was Barbara Mills, and the *Herald* reported on her memories:

> She tells how when she was 11 years old her family was wiped out and she was 'pulled from her own grave' after the shelter took a direct hit. The blast was so huge that some bodies were unidentifiable; human remains were found in the tops of trees and around the square. Incredibly, Barbara only suffered minor cuts.

She was one of just three survivors. The paper added:

> On the night her family died, air-raid sirens alerted the family to yet another onslaught by German bombers which had been pounding the city for days. They took refuge in the public shelter; her grandfather was a shelter warden. Her last glimpse of her bus conductor father was as he polished the buttons of his uniform.

Tony Wood has written a book on the whole terrible episode, and in the *Herald* he explained why the memorial was so important:

> My fear was that as the university campus continued to expand, the site's history would be swallowed up and lost. If city residents come up with the money, the memorial sculpture – depicting an adult holding up a child, to represent the rebirth of Plymouth – will be placed on the spot where the shelter stood, at the centre of the university campus.

The sculptor is Frances May Favata, who used her son-in-law and grandchildren for the production of the design. She told the press: 'I wanted to make a statement about the tenacity of the Plymouth people.' In the programme for the launch event, Frances Favata wrote:

> When war occurs the adults' instinct is often to save our children. They are the future...I developed the idea of an adult lifting up a child with this in mind. The distortion that war brings to our lives and communities is expressed through the curved stainless steel panels behind the sculpture.

All this has come from the worst fear of shelter life – the distant chance of a direct hit – but then, long shots do sometimes happen, and Plymouth was unfortunate in the extreme on that dreadful night.

Our museums and heritage projects are, as these examples show, working hard to make history 'real'. The usual gory exhibits such as the skeletons of highwaymen or the gibbets used for the punishment of horrible murderers may have drawn the public in, but now these have rivals – the tales from the shelters.

Laughs and Books
The experience of shelter life was not always dour and uncomfortable, though. Brian Callan has a more light-hearted and bizarre memory of being in the Anderson one night at the height of a raid:

We had a dog, Roddy, an amiable sheep-dog type. He liked nothing more than a late-night air-raid because it meant an unexpected walk in the dark. We, that is, mother and granddad, plus the Whitworth family, who did not have a shelter of their own, would run down to the shelter when the siren went and Roddy would take himself off to do whatever dogs do during night-time walkies. Dad was in the Civil Defence Heavy Rescue Squad so he was usually on duty during air-raids. Because we were well to the west of Hull, most raids were some distance away and not too frightening, only exciting.

On the night of Roddy's adventure in April 1942, we all gathered at the shelter and as usual, Roddy took himself off. We suddenly heard the sound of an aircraft. 'It's one of theirs,' said granddad... We all listened; suddenly there was the unmistakeable sound of a bomb falling towards us. I remember all of us bending double in our seats and covering our ears. There was an enormous explosion and the ground shook – total silence seemed to follow. We lifted our heads and heard, distinctly, a strange scrambling noise coming from outside – it was Roddy hurtling down the concrete path! At high speed, he burst into the shelter and stood, in the candlelight, trembling with fear. Before anyone had chance to speak, there was a loud rasping, bubbling noise and Roddy emptied what must have been the entire contents of his bowels with great violence in the corner of the shelter, next to granddad...

Roddy became one of the most notorious characters of the Blitz after that around that street. Bizarre though the tale is, it exemplifies so many unpleasant yet laughable sidelights to the terror.

We know about shelter life from pictorial sources as well as from the written word and from spoken memories. Freelance photographer Marvin Breckinridge Patterson took the first pictures of a London air-raid shelter. The journalist, Ed Murrow employed her as a staff reporter for his London-based CBS outfit. Patterson made broadcasts from various locations in Europe. With her camera, she also set about documenting the everyday life in the war. Her picture of the Savoy Hotel shelter is a rare image of the wealthier end of life in the Blitz: men sit in semi-darkness, wearing silk dressing-gowns, while couples wearing flowery dresses and blazers chat. A warden stands with them, and a man who wears what appears to be a naval officer's hat. Behind them are piles of sandbags alongside the ornate columns of the hotel's architecture.

The shelters did not mean that brainwork and the intellectual life of the nation had to be put on hold. *The Times Crossword Book* for the New Year of 1941 made that clear:

> The lenitive influence of the crossword puzzle is not without importance in total warfare. It soothes the passing hours of the blackout which the people have learnt to spend at home, and still more, the time that is spent in air-raid shelters. *The Times Crossword Puzzle Book* is accordingly a very rare addition to the list of Penguin Books … It is estimated that this book should give the average solver anything from 50 to 200 hours of concentrated mental gymnastics…

This concern for entertainment and culture in the shelters spread to *The Manchester Guardian*, even before the bombs came. In 1938 that paper ran a competition inviting readers to send in a list with reasons for the compilation, of 'six books with which to furnish a gas–proof room'. A report on this said:

> The competitor from Ulverston who suggested Bacon's *Novum Organum*, *The Last Days of Pompeii*, *The City of Dreadful Night* and *Paradise Lost* … presumably knows his own mind better than anyone else does, but most people would say that the furniture of such a room

would only be complete with a revolver to be used in case the gas and bombs and literature all failed to do their work.

But there were very practical suggestions:

> The books must steady jittery nerves by distracting the mind from business overhead. Whilst entertainment is required, purely light literature is useless, since it does not demand sufficient concentration. Humour only irritates in moments of strain. Books giving something to do are therefore best...

Some readers made suggestions with a real purpose: 'Rabelais... for a reminder that there are better kinds of nonsense than dropping bombs.' One of the most sustained lists, and with clear meanings, came from a Mr Douglas Rawson. His books included *The Anatomy of Melancholy* 'for general reading'; phrase books for Italian and German 'in case of visitors'; a family Bible 'exhibiting Aryan descent' and a students' song book for community singing. *The Guardian* eventually concluded:

> But perhaps in the end we should all be pessimists enough to reach out automatically for Jeremy Taylor's *Holy Living and Holy Dying*. Its advantage is, of course, that, supposing the precautions did work after all, we could concentrate on the first half.

Games such as chess and draughts were very popular. Writing after the war, one writer to *The Evening Standard* said of chess:

> The game itself has remained a solace to many through war, as it has been since the Crusades. It has been played with pocket sets on the battlefield; it has whiled away long hours in the air-raid shelters and fire wardens in the darkness on city roofs have been known to play by word of mouth.

Naturally, there were songs. Songs and jokes were in high demand in all kinds of places, and nobody worried too much about quality – enthusiasm was the thing. The radio character, Jack Davey, recorded a song called 'Our Air Raid Shelter' in April 1942, expressing some of the salient features of life under cover, including these verses:

Of course it isn't very big, and it isn't very long,
And it isn't very deep, and it isn't very strong.
So if a bomb drops take a quick look up at heaven
For Aunt 'n' Dad 'n' Gran 'n' Dad 'n' Mum 'n' me.

Old granny's causing us concern, though she doesn't care a bit,
For her bustle sticks outside and may get a direct hit.
And if she pulls it in it makes it worse than ever,
For Aunt 'n' her 'n' Dad 'n' Mum and me ...

There was a determined effort by the media to paint a picture of shelter life as being not entirely miserable. When Wendell Willkie, a nominee for the 1940 American presidential election, visited London, *The Times* reported:

Mr Willkie visited five shelters, including one of the biggest in East London. At each shelter he was loudly cheered by people, who chanted, 'Are we down-hearted? No!' As he travelled from shelter to shelter Mr Willkie heard the noise of gunfire and droning of aircraft and saw flashes light up the night sky. Afterwards, Mr Willkie stated that he chatted with many people in the shelters and found it a most stimulating experience. He found no-one depressed. It was a most moving thing to see all these people underground, of necessity congested, and yet their spirit was wonderful.

Merton Paul was in Manchester in the war, and he recalls their shelter and some attempts at entertainment:

It was always very cold in the shelter ... so I used to wear a siren suit ... I would leap out of bed at the sound of a siren and jump into my suit and hurry to the shelter ... we had a record player which had to be wound up by hand. We used to play records. I clearly remember the records by Flanagan and Allen entitled 'Umbrella Man' and 'Underneath the Arches'. The air-raid shelter was basically a square hole in the ground covered by corrugated iron sheets. We all had gas masks in little cardboard boxes with a piece of string so you could carry it over your shoulder ...

604

Chelsea Pensioners in the Wars Again

CHELSEA ROYAL HOSPITAL, home of the famous Chelsea Pensioners, suffered damage as the result of one of the intensive night raids on London by the enemy. The Royal Hospital, which was founded during the reign of Charles II, was designed by Sir Christopher Wren and opened in 1694. This well-known institution was one of the first of its kind for old and disabled soldiers left alone in the world. The Hospital accommodates about 550 " in-pensioners " as distinguished from " out-pensioners." There is also accommodation for six officers, who are known as Captains of Invalids.

CHELSEA PENSIONER, H. A. Rattray, circle, aged one hundred, was in the Hospital when it was bombed, but the Nazis could not subdue his spirits. Result of bomb damage is seen above. A hole was torn in the wall of one of the buildings, causing damage to all five floors.

Pensioners safe in Wren's Great Hall. (The War Illustrated, *1940*)

Taking a wider view of things, we can see that the reality behind this was one in which the British excelled: the stiff upper lip. The oral history testifies well that the spirit of survival was the usual earthy mix of living by sayings and phrases immersed in the human comedy – something reinforced every day by the comics on the radio – something counterbalancing the serious clipped voice reminders of duty and responsibility coming from politicians and officials. The motto 'Get your message through' meant that channels of communication were essential, and both for messages and for laughs in the face of adversity. Finding ways to lighten the situation required all kinds of enterprise and invention, and the stories show that people developed rare skills in these kinds of activities, since labelled 'making do'.

Doreen Hodges has a memory of a good time down a school shelter:

> There were some shelters at Hartfield Crescent School – it was awkward to descend down the straight ladder ... However, when we did get down the teacher started a whispering game to help us pass the time. It started like this: 'Three little sausages sizzling in the frying-pan'. By the time it had gone all the way round it ended in a giggle ...

For most, it was a case of instinctive attempts to keep cheerful, as Alison North reports of her mother's memories:

> She was about 6 years old when the war started and she and her family had to sleep for many nights in their Anderson shelter in Wyton Grove [Hull] wearing siren suits and used to sing along, joining in with their neighbours in the next-door shelter, to keep themselves from worrying.

As the lives of Gracie Fields and Vera Lynn show very clearly, there is nothing quite like a good tuneful song to boost morale. In the school sing-songs, nobody worried about the quality: it was the spirit of it that counted.

Of course, shelter humour found its way into literature too, and typical is Spike Milligan's joke:

> *My mother was digging an air-raid shelter.*
> *'She's a great little woman,' said my father.*
> *'Getting smaller and smaller all the time,' said I.*

Many of the stories collected here include tales of family members being too late to get to the shelter, or of people running back inside the house to fetch precious possessions. One memory typifies this:

> We were all in, and we had got there in such a rush that nobody had realised that little Tom was still in his bedroom and that Charlie, his dog, was with him. I dashed back in and I heard this barking and yelping – as it was so noisy and frightening – and Charlie had gone under the bed, and there was Tom trying to drag him out by his tail. I shouted, 'Thomas, get yourself down here now. Leave the bloody dog!' Then when we were all down there, Tom says that Daddy swore. 'I bloody didn't,' I said.

The author Edgar Rice Burroughs, creator of 'Tarzan', played his part in raising a laugh in the war. In 1942 he wrote a column called 'Laugh it Off' for the *Honolulu Star*. Typical of this is his tale of a deluxe shelter:

> A private air-raid shelter I recently inspected, which will accommodate twenty or thirty people, has a ventilating fan, electric lights, radio, a raised plank floor with Morocco leather cushions, cigarettes, ice, Scotch, soda and water. There was no food, but then we all have to make sacrifices during wartime.

But far more evident were the tales of farce, as in this crazy story from Edith Kay of Bolton, when interviewed by Ken Beevers:

> My auntie used to come and stay with us when there was an air-raid because she was expecting her first baby...and I can remember it really startled her and she fell off a stepladder near the...you know... We used to go down a couple of steps and she used to sit there. She was always a very jolly person...when that bomb dropped she just fell off...

It was the ladder she fell off, and we assume that she landed on the makeshift toilet.

Getting Spiritual
There is no doubt that for some, the shelter was a strange place, somewhere between a cell and a retreat for meditation. Others went so far

as to have mystical experiences in them, as the Romanian cultural attaché in London, Mircea Eliade, wrote in his autobiography:

> When, on the night of September 9, 1940, we descended into the London air-raid shelter from the fifth floor of the building where one of my colleagues from the Romanian legation lived, remembered suddenly – instantaneously, as though they consisted of a single episode – a great many things that had happened to me in the past three years. The sensation was so strange that I said to myself that, very probably, I would not come out of that shelter alive. I don't know if I was afraid or not. But seeing several children there, I had difficulty resisting the temptation to go over and urge their parents to leave with them as quickly as possible while there was still time...

He does not record if his presentiment was right or not, but the point is that he expressed something of that fatalistic line of thought felt by so many in the Blitz.

Keeping Records

People did keep their own documents, of course. Many realised that they were living through an extraordinary time in history, and they felt that things had to be logged, annotated and described in some way. Some drew sketches; some wrote poems; others simply wrote lists. Sometimes these notes were of the most mundane kind, but as time has passed, they have attained a special place in written and recorded social history. Of course, it was a time of privations, so people used whatever material came to hand. Drawers and cupboards and attics were searched for anything that could be of use. In an age of documentary, almost everyone joined in this activity, so now across the land we have numerous personal archives, tucked away gathering dust. Fortunately, we are now revisiting this horrendous time, and learning what it was like to live under such conditions.

The amazing aspect of all this is that ordinary folk somehow knew that what was happening was truly momentous and that it should be preserved, in its smallest features.

One truly remarkable piece of recorded history from the Blitz was from Mrs Vera James, a housewife who kept a meticulous record, day by day, of bombings in an old 'Laboratory Notebook' from 1922. Here is a random sample of her entries:

1940
Mon. 11.50 p.m.– 12.55 a.m. Bombs H. E. Porter Street
Th.   1.15 p.m. – 2.30 p.m. Machine-gun fire (after balloons)
Sat. 10.35 p.m.– 10.50 p.m. Bomb H E Holderness Road, Morrill St.
1941
Sun. 7.10 p.m. – 1.00 a.m. Gunfire, bombs Willerby and Sutton
Sun. H and A wedding. At church.
      Guns, Telford Street.
Sun. Shrapnel fell in drive
Wed. Goddard Avenue – bombs

(H E = High Explosive bombs)

Her son, Trevor, has preserved the notebook, and he also notes that the diary records what his mother was baking, in between the bombs and guns.

Experience of shelters was always mixed:

The next night we went to Tooting underground…Hundreds of people were down there laying on platforms. We had to find ourselves a place to lay our pillow and blanket and there we sat, fed up and miserable. We could have wept, if we hadn't seen the funny side of it.

So Ethel Robinson recalled, and the last sentence sums up the general attitude. Margaret Clark's memory is equally one of a frenetic and slightly absurd experience:

We used to run down to Clapham North Tube station…It was my duty, as you might say, to hold this old music case with the insurance policies, half a bottle of brandy (for medicinal purposes) and all things like that. All the family papers, birth certificates as well. That was my job. I had to grab that when we ran off somewhere.

In most of the air-raid stories there is some humour. Reading these accounts today, one feels that the kind of *Carry On* film humour is not far from the truth when it sets about defining the British attitudes to stress and strain. Rod Fennings' family story defines this precisely:

Sid, who was only used to the normal bombing and fighting that occurred in the Egyptian desert, ran in from outside the house shouting, 'What the bloody hell is that?' and he shoved himself under the table in the kitchen. Quickly realising that there was no-one else to be seen, he promptly went running down into the cellar with a large pan covering his head. My mother, who was used to these severe air-raids said to Sid, 'What on earth is the matter? It's only an air-raid.' To which Sid replied that it was safer in the desert.

Joe Somerville's memory is of family chaos too:

I was 6 years old in 1940 and our family lived in Hornchurch, Essex. Our dear old dad was home on leave at the time the air-raid siren went off. Dad had taken us all down into the shelter and then said 'Where's your Gran?' He looked round and she was not in the shelter. He called out, 'Come down here Ma, there are German planes up there!' She called back, 'I can't come yet son, I'm looking for my teeth!' Dad went up to get her and shouted, 'Get down in the shelter…they're dropping bombs, not bloody pork pies!'

This brand of humour makes it clear that in reality the dogged humour of those under fire was something akin to the supposed spoofs of British grit in the Pinewood Studios films.

Jean Clayton was born in 1940 but still has a shelter tale to tell:

I can remember going down the air-raid shelters with my auntie and my mother. They would be carrying lights with paraffin in and candles. Sometimes we stayed down the shelters for what seemed like hours. I think I must have been about 3 years old then. My mother told me I was born in a little two-up, two-down cottage next to an old library in Margate in Kent. She told me she heard a bomb coming down, which probably sounded like it was overhead, anyway she told me she got out of bed and went underneath it for safety.

Eddie Gardner recalls the fear of being inside, but still close to the action:

It was about 5.20 p.m. 16th August 1940 and I was one of about twenty-two young people in an air-raid shelter outside our place of work and beside the Kingston by-pass (A3). The usual chatter in the shelter stopped as the anti-aircraft guns opened up and suddenly a series of explosions took place. The young shelter warden cried out, 'It's all right, it's only our guns opening up,' and this settled many of the people in the shelter but I knew that the sudden suction of dust from the shelter indicated a bomb explosion … Inwardly I was shaking like a jelly but I tried not to show my fear …

Comfort?

Naturally, trying to make the unwelcoming shelters as comfortable as possible was a real challenge. The columnist Mary Rose of the *Daily Sketch* had lots of suggestions in August 1940:

> I find that a travelling rug is a grand thing for keeping out the cold on chilly evenings. So is a hot water bottle if you have constant hot water … One mother I know takes a flask of hot water to the shelter and makes her two boys hot drinks with fruit syrup. Smelling salts and eau de cologne are always good to have handy. They freshen you up so.

Mary was always informed of the latest trends and goods available, such as in her unashamed product placements:

> Atkinson's of Bond Street have just produced a little case containing a bottle of their gold medal eau de cologne and six of their famous Freshettes, complete with waterproof envelope to hold each Freshette while it is in use for 1s and 9d. They also have special little air-raid shelter packs containing a small bottle of eau de cologne and a bottle of smelling salts …

Dealing with undesirable smells was a common problem. One story that has come down in oral history is of a woman who had a little gem in her antiques collection – a vinaigrette from around 1840. In this gorgeous little silver box, with its pad which people would have soaked with something sweet-smelling, she used to put lavender oil. But one day the lavender supplies ran out. 'I asked my daughter to put something nice-smelling in there … she did all right – it was Dettol. I took a sniff, expecting something floral, and the sniff almost knocked me out.'

KEEP THE GLAMOUR OF A YOUTHFUL SKIN

NEVER let the years steal your birthright of a youthful skin. Nature meant your complexion to be renewed and refreshed with every day that passed. She meant the drying outer skin imperceptibly to dissolve and to make way for the fresh new skin which is always growing underneath.

But for most women modern life has ruined Nature's plan. Tiny particles of the old dead skin remain to clog the pores and choke the life of the tender skin below.

You can restore Nature's power easily, simply, certainly. Just get from your chemist some pure Mercolized Wax and gently rub it in with the finger-tips before you go to bed. While you sleep the Mercolized Wax will be softly, imperceptibly dissolving away all those tiny particles of old worn-out skin leaving the fresh young skin underneath healthy, clear and beautiful.

Even one night will show you how this natural way transcends all artificial means and lotions. But be sure to get Mercolized Wax and follow the instructions on the jar. Price 2/- and 3/6.

Send for copy of "Lessons in Loveliness."
post free.

DEARBORN (1923) LTD., 37, GRAY'S INN ROAD, LONDON, W.C.1.

MERCOLIZED WAX

DOES NOT contain Mercury, animal fat, or anything injurious to the complexion, and is guaranteed not to encourage the growth of hair.

Making the best of a "Sheltered" *Life*

IN these times when the sirens call us up so often from our nice w a r m beds, t h e shelter has become a very important part of o u r homes, and most of u s h a v e learned b y experi e n c e what a number of little things we can do to add to

By Mary Rose

its comfort.

Some people find it most restful to lie down, and it's a grand idea to put a nice warm rug on the floor if you haven't a Li-Lo and there's no room for a small mattress, and cover yourself up with your eiderdown.

Then, with two pillows on which to rest your head, you can doze away to your heart's content until the "all clear" sounds.

In one shelter I know the man of the family has built up two regular steamer cabin beds at one end for his two small children. Another "handyman" has made a grand "sleeper" for baby in his shelter.

★   ★   ★

FOR a very small sum he bought an old tennis net and utilised the best parts to make a miniature hammock; rings securely fixed to the roof and two meat hooks complete the outfit, and in a trice baby is "slung up" out of the way, quite happily swinging in his hammock. I find that a travelling rug is a grand thing for keeping out the cold on chilly evenings. So is a hot-water

laid on from which it can be filled quickly.

One mother I know takes a flask of hot water to the shelter and makes her two boys hot drinks with fruit syrup. Smelling-salts and eau-de-cologne are always good to have handy. They freshen you up so. Atkinson's of Bond - street have just produced a little case containing a bottle of their gold medal eau-de-cologne and six of their famous Freshettes, complete with water-proof envelope, to hold each Freshette while it is in use, for 1s. 9d.

They also have special little air raid shelter packs containing a small bottle of eau-de-cologne and a small bottle of smelling salts.

ANY IDEAS?

HAVE you any ideas for adding to the comfort of your shelter? If so, I shall be pleased to have them to pass on to other readers.

Your Badge

Have you sent for your badge yet? If not, let me have your name and address straight away and I will tell you how you can get it and become a member of my Housewives' League. The badge is quite free, and my address is MARY ROSE, Housewives' League, "Daily Sketch," 196, Gray's Inn-road, London, W.C.1.

Mary Rose's column from the *Daily Sketch*, 1940.

Mary Rose and her column were part of something very important in the dissemination of advice and knowledge then: the housewife. Mary had her own Housewives' League and members could send for a badge. Any tips for shelter life were welcome: it was ideal for anyone with a *Blue Peter* turn of mind. If someone could send in a suggestion for a little help or comfort, that was just the thing that would earn her a badge. How many ladies sat in shelters showing off Mary Rose badges is something yet to be ascertained. But the illustration for her column shows women enjoying a cuppa while a man smiles and smokes a pipe in the background – clearly there were no worries then about the dangers of passive smoking in enclosed spaces. Pipe-smoking was seen as cosy, rather than as a danger to health.

As usual, the British did what they were always good at: making the best of a bad job, and then settling in. Phrases dominated conversation: 'For the duration…' and 'Look, no butter!' The cartoonists and humorists did their best to cheer everyone up in the face of horror.

Interesting Variations

People tried to add a little comfort in all kinds of ways. Some people had skills that were very relevant to the construction of their own shelters, and so there were a number of highly original ones on record. Such a case was that shelter built by ex-miner Tommy Hart. In a photo taken when he was 100 years old, he is seen standing next to his pride and joy – a mound with a rockery over the top and a wooden, green-painted door with a latch. His profession gave him the right kind of ability to make this shelter a home from home, and it must have been the pride of Herringthorpe, near Rotherham.

The Morris bed-type shelter designed by the Bolton firm. (*Courtesy of Mr R J Maxwell*)

Specialists of all kinds got to work to make their own varieties. R J Maxwell has written to explain that his father, owner of Robert Morris Ltd., made an indoor version to rival that of the Morrison type. Mr Maxwell writes:

> My late father designed at first a corrugated table top type for indoors, in September 1940 and an outdoor one later, then finally an indoor one in January 1941 which we used at home throughout the war. This last design was most successful in saving lives in the Manchester Blitz.

Mr Maxwell has kept the archive of original drawings. The photo of the 'bed-type' Morris shelter shows an arched cover with bolts fixing the strong panels in place, and inside is a mattress and cover. It looks very snug and comfortable.

Shelter of any kind would be commandeered in emergencies, of course. Ken Bowskill recalls one very strange make-do refuge:

> Employees used to be conned into staying on the premises at night on fire watch. One night I was on duty and it was very cold so I found a warm spot, in a coffin. I fell asleep (quiet night) and a door was opened by the local Air Raid Warden. I popped my head up and the guy saw me complete with warm shroud then took off, leaving a nasty smell. Apparently the curtains weren't closed properly and a chink of light was showing.

A Feast Down Below?

Of course, the war was an age of rationing. The man called in to organise this was a Manchester businessman called Frederick Marquis, later to be Lord Woolton, a socialist in his younger days. He was to become Uncle Fred generally, and as Terry Charman wrote in an article in *The Independent* in 2010, 'He took the public into his confidence, warning them of impending shortages, and frankly admitting and correcting the occasional errors of judgement and maladministration by his Ministry.' Rationing then began – on 8 January 1940 and ration books were everywhere. Cooking fats and teas were rationed at first, and then jam and cheese.

But however much there was a food shortage, many made a special effort to take some kind of food down into the shelter. Home baking was paramount; many made treats such as jam tarts and cake (though these were cakes without egg or much else). When accidents happened there was big trouble. One woman told the tale of a large jar of jam being carried home and then being dropped. The jar smashed and the glass splintered and shattered. The girl and her friend tried to pick out bits of strawberry preserve from among the glass but to no avail. Eventually they returned home without the jam, and they had to take the anger that waited for them.

There was always tea, in spite of the rationing. Although the size of a slice of bread was supposed to be checked against a chart, the effort to make do was successful, and if nothing else, food in shelters, however meagre, was cheery. Tea, bread and butter were still the standard fare. Eating and drinking became collective: a sign of the times was the announcement of a pig club at the zoo:

A pig club has been started at the zoo. Thirty members of staff, including a number of keepers, have now added pigs to their charges. The zoo restaurant will be able to make bacon from its saved waste and the pig club has been placed on the boundary of the zoo and Regent's Park where the general public can take an active interest in it.

A chat in semi-darkness, with some tea from a flask perhaps, and maybe some family memories, meant that the war years were a time rich in oral storytelling. Speakers, singers and entertainers had a captive audience.

Elbow Room

Hitler might have been droning on about 'room to live' for his new Aryan nation, and so expanding into other countries' land was his habit, but in England, long before war broke out, there were numerous poor people who were quite used to living in areas the size of a public shelter. It was a matter of rich and poor. When George Orwell set out to visit and write about the northern workers and others in his book, *The Road to Wigan Pier* (published in 1937) he made a point of describing such things, as he did when writing about families living in old caravans: 'One, for instance, measuring 14 feet long, had seven people in it ... which is to say that each person had for his entire dwelling space a good deal smaller than one compartment of a public lavatory ...'

So for some, public shelters must have seemed like a vast space, until they filled up and people settled in. However, the point is that they provided an available space, and the potential was infinite. John Perry wrote that he knew a very unusual use:

Some deep shelters were put into place in Watford and these were dug quite deeply with two flights of steps going down. They were very well constructed because several were used as fitness training areas until a long time after the Second World War. I attended one that was a weight-lifting training club. They were not at all damp and must have been well tanked to keep them dry.

The Show Must Go On

One of the best examples of British determination to get involved and see things through in spite of the *Luftwaffe* comes from a report by the theatre critic W A Darlington, at Christmas 1940. He wrote:

The Pilgrim Players were due to give a lunch-time performance of Charles Williams' nativity play in verse, *The House by the Stable* in a City church. When I arrived, picking my way among firemen's hoses, the church was there minus its windows, which had been blown out by a high-explosive bomb, and the company was there, all but one archangel. So was the nucleus of an audience. The missing archangel was in charge of the van with the costumes and might not be able to find a way around roped-off streets in time…Players and audience parted with mutual regret, the players to find some other building – church, air-raid shelter or what you will – in which the play may be given.

The men in suits who spent their time working out morale-boosting propaganda would have loved that. The best kind of morale-boosting art is that which causes a smile while at the same time making a point about 'true grit' – and yet the media loved to suggest that it was British eccentricity and doggedness that was the best propaganda. As many Americans commented at the time, 'The British are so crazy that they fool themselves into thinking they can't lose, and that means they won't.' This was not entirely off the mark; there was an attitude of resilience. As one woman recently told the press: 'When somebody wants to take something you have and you won't give it, then you fight to the death, and we were willing to do just that.'

Let Loose the Dogs of War

Of course, pets were not allowed in the shelters. But there were some heroes of the canine kind and some bizarre tales of people and dogs in the raids. In America, Parks Johnson of Great Neck, Long Island made a shelter especially for dogs, including the essential provisions of water, canned meat and dog biscuits in the underground den. In Britain, the boffins got to work on all kinds of technical difficulties, and sure enough, Marcus le Touche of Charlton invented a gas-proof shelter for dogs – he insisted that it was entirely safe from poisonous fumes.

In the category of problems caused by dogs, we have Jimmy Boyle's story from Glasgow:

> On one of these fine days in the summer of '44 I had an urgency to hide in my local shelter … this little terrier dog took a fancy to my leg so I gave him a screamer of a kick … only for him to growl and snarl viciously towards my personal parts. Now he was going to bite me as well as *furnicate* me. No way, I thought, as I shot into the shelter in the middle of the street.

The dog followed Jimmy:

> He got me in one but like my hero Flash Gordon I kicked him and he ran screaming like a wee girl. When I awoke in the Royal Infirmary after my week-long coma I thought to myself that wee yin can fairly fight. The moral of this story is that I should have played down the other shelter.

The shelters also had their canine heroes, none so famous as the great Rip, who went scrabbling for people trapped under rubble. He found over 100 people in his time and that was achieved without any official training in the work: he had been given no rescue training, but was simply a 'natural'. In 1945 he was decorated, being given a medal by Maria Dickin, who created the awards, which were given to dogs, pigeons, horses, and once, even to a cat. In 2009 his medal was sold for $35,700.

Rip and his colleagues achieved great things. In 1944 when the doodlebugs came, a typical action by rescue dogs did wonderful service, as *The Times* reported:

> In another incident a young woman living in a row of houses which was hit by a V bomb owed her life to two RAF rescue dogs. For more than four hours after the bomb fell the dogs worked along the row. They stopped on a pile of rubble and barked excitedly. After digging for ten minutes and scarcely believing it possible that anybody could be alive under it, rescue workers came to a Morrison shelter and found the woman inside. She had only minor injuries but was almost suffocated. Several persons were killed and a number injured.

In January 1945 a doodlebug hit a building and shelter and the dogs were called out again. They managed to find survivors, with the assistance of searchlights. This was a common occurrence and people were familiar with the sight of the dogs working in the rubble. When the victory parade took place in 1946, the rescue dogs were walking with the people, and their presence was, as we would expect in England, very popular with the spectators.

Chapter 9

'Mum heard a Doodlebug': Amazing Tales

'The south-east of Kent became known as Bomb Alley...'
Violet Apted

In early June 1944 the Allies were landing in Normandy. D-Day had begun. Yet further along the French coast and into Holland, Hitler had a line of special installations in place, buried beneath the earth and hard to find. These were the nests of the infamous 'doodlebugs' – properly known as V1s from the German *Vergeltungswaffe Eins*, 'Revenge Weapon Number One'. On 13 June, at the break of day, two men in Kent saw the first doodlebug appear. It was a black shape with a red spray of light behind it. Was it a fighter? Was it a rocket? There had been talk of Hitler's secret weapon, and this was the prototype.

Three more days passed before the general public were informed about these strange new weapons in the sky. Soon after, several rockets reached London. Violet Apted has spoken about the experience of these mysterious threats from above:

> Chills of horror, wearing hobnail boots, ran up and down my spine when I saw my first doodlebug. It was the night science fiction became a reality to the children of the UK... We had moved into our new house after being bombed out of our previous home... My bed was placed under a long window and became a box seat for all of us to watch the nightly air-raid 'shows'. How could we have known, tonight would be so different!

Violet described the object: '... there it was, a long cigar-shaped object with stubby wings held in the glow of a searchlight beam. Flames were spewing out of the back of it. Then there was another and another...' She said that the south-east of Kent became known as Bomb Alley during the next eighty days of V1 and then V2 rocket attacks.

Ron Moore recalls an event during the doodlebug year which is somewhere between tragedy and farce:

> Then came the doodlebugs. When the siren went they were mostly over Croydon so I had to stand on top of the Anderson shelter and blow a whistle if I saw one, and all the neighbours ran for the shelter. One day we had the first of the season's new peas and the dinner was just put on the table, and a doodlebug landed nearby and exploded. The entire ceiling came down on top of the dinner. We were very angry at Mr Hitler. Unfortunately, my poor old dad had arthritis...he could only get to the doorway...the ceiling came down but he was not hurt...

It was as if the science fiction tales in the magazines had suddenly come true: yes, there were metal monsters up there, maybe created by mad doctors; they really did come over you in the very ordinary skies of everyday life and threaten death. It was a nightmare, seemingly out of *Boy's Own* comic but crashing into reality like the evil world of the adventure stories and dystopias.

These flying bombs were to kill almost 23,000 people, and over 8,000 of them were launched against London. One of the most informative

A doodlebug. (*Author's collection*)

accounts we have comes from Vera Hodgson, who kept a diary. She refers to the craft as 'robots':

> By Saturday we all felt very cheap. I longed to go and see the Invasion pictures, but did not feel equal to cope with the queues – so went to a local cinema ... All through we had across the screen AIR RAID WARNING. Then 'All Clear'. Three times. But the audience was in a light-hearted mood and laughed aloud. We had not learned to take the Robots seriously ... Went along Marloes Road ... Heavy Rescue lorries were driving in and gathering up debris. All one roof of the hospital gone. One woman and twelve children were brought out dead ...

Technical Description

The Nazi cruise missile weighed 4,750lb and had a wingspan of 17 feet 6 inches. Its speed was 393 mph and it had a range of 1,250 miles, operating at an altitude of between 2,000 and 3,000 feet. It had been developed at Peenemunde in Germany by Robert Lusser and Fritz Gosslau. The V1 was a welded sheet-metal fuselage with plywood wings. Its Argus jet engine had an intake vane system. The warhead was full of high explosive and the detonator was placed in a chamber behind the nose.

The tube that people saw mounted on top, at the rear, was where the jet engine was, with the air intake vanes. In the tail section there was a rudder and also an elevator. Germany made around 30,000 of these monsters, manufactured with the use of slave labour at an underground factory near Nordhausen.

First-Hand Experience

Violet Apted and her family used their shelter for the first time when the doodlebugs came:

> Suddenly the jets of flame coming from the doodlebugs cut off. They plummeted to the ground and exploded. Mum rushed us all downstairs and out into the Anderson air-raid shelter in the back garden. That was the first and only time we used the shelter, but this was an unknown danger and Mum wanted to be sure what it was, so made sure we were safe.

Colin Wilson's father was stationed at RAF Chigwell and the family had rented a house at Hornchurch. He wrote:

> Mum had put me in my pram in the back garden when she heard a doodlebug. She came back outside just as the damned thing cut out! She ran down the garden and grabbed me out of the pram and dashed towards the Anderson shelter at the end of the garden. Unfortunately the smock she was wearing somehow got caught around the handle of the pram and so she threw me and herself into the shelter – the pram came too! The doodlebug landed a few hundred yards away, causing colossal damage.

These monsters certainly did some damage. One person recalls:

> One early morning… Mum took us down Faraday Road and we saw then ten houses had been knocked down the night before by a doodlebug. The road was cordoned off and the heavy squad were at work. This bomb had also seriously damaged the back corner of our school in Effra Road. We kids were fairly cheerful about that.

One correspondent refers to the doodlebugs as 'cheap, crude, scruffy little weapons'. But they certainly instilled fear. Victor Spink noted that the Morrison shelters came into their own then:

> Some of the mums in our road went out and did part-time jobs, so the arrangement was that the mums who were in their homes would leave their front doors open so we kids playing in the road could run into the first open door near to where we were playing and dive under the steel Morrison table shelter in the dining room, dog and all. The mothers who were off work would just naturally look after all of the street's kids who played together.

Again, the Boy Scouts were busy and very much involved. Jack Sammons has written about his time in the Scouts at this point:

> Soon after the war started Senior Boy Scouts were recruited as War Service Scouts and helped in many ways. We wore yellow armbands when collecting waste paper, putting up bright propaganda posters and

covering up broken windows after the doodlebugs and V2s began to reach north London. I was with the 2nd Kenton Troop and our Scoutmaster Don Pettit set up our HQ in his garden shed, complete with telephone. We had calls to erect Morrison shelters. These comprised four angle-iron corner posts connected at the top with long angle-iron strips. The roof to the shelter was a huge heavy metal sheet with holes drilled around the edges. The difficulty was to match the holes in the metal sheet with those in the angle-iron connectors using brute force. All this was achieved in small furnished living rooms.

V2s – Doodlebugs Mark 2

Hitler's second 'revenge' rocket was the V2. These were sent over London in the autumn of 1944. This was the world's first ballistic missile, and over 1,400 were sent towards London. The rocket had a 13-tonne burden and this time, there was no warning. Air-raid shelter protection did not figure largely in this last phase of war bombing. On a website called 'Londonist' (see Bibliography), a map has been made of all the V2 strikes. The deadly statistics that go with this are as follows:

> Some 9,000 Londoners lost their lives ... Some did make it into central areas ... V2 explosions devastated Selfridges, Speakers' Corner and Holborn. That isolated Caffè Nero near the mural on Tottenham Court Road stands on the still-undeveloped site of a blast that killed nine ... The worst death toll of all came on 25 November 1944, when 168 people lost their lives after a direct hit on Woolworths in New Cross.

The V2 was a tragedy for the workers at the German end, too: over 20,000 inmates of the Mittelbau-Dora plant died during the construction work. The rocket was in service from September 1944 to the end of the war, and was first produced in March 1942. Hitler had grand designs for annihilating Britain after such a long and ultimately pointless bombing campaign with orthodox weapons. His scientists had been at work on the new rocket for some time, notably Wernher von Braun, who started tests on liquid-driven rockets. He was given a research grant, and he and others had, before the war, asked the American scientist Robert Goddard for advice.

Like the V1, the V2 was guided by rudders at the fins and the first ones used a computer. The crucial factor was the timing of the engine shut-off. This was controlled by a ground control system. After test launches in Sweden the Allies knew about this infernal machine and after that there were flights across the Channel to try to destroy the launch pads. This was very important work: it was possible to launch around 1,000 V2s a month.

The bombings were terrible. One memory records a horrific result of one bomb:

> A lady next to me was practically stripped of her clothes, all in a heap, and next to her was a girl, evidently killed instantaneously. On the other side a gentleman, evidently with a broken back, for whom I made a rest for his head with a piece of wood and two bricks…

Robin Dale, of Essex, has spoken about the V1 and its distinctive sound:

> One day mum sent me to Manningtree to pick up a prescription from Lyons the chemist. I reckon I broke the cycle record for the 6-mile trip. I admit I was terrified. The characteristic noise of the 'Ram jet' is imprinted on my mind, listening to them in bed and waiting for the engine to stop. I recollect seeing just a couple of those horrors; one went over a bungalow at about 1,000 feet, belching fire. I banged my head getting under the bed! Then there was one which destroyed the church at Chelmondiston.

On Boxing Day 1944 a Mr and Mrs Streeter's pub, the Prince of Wales, was hit by a V2. The death toll was sixty-nine people. Survivors recorded walking to a rest centre, where they were given clothes. After that it was a long recovery, and plenty of post-traumatic stress, though that phrase did not exist at the time. There was little anyone could do. The most well-mediated direct hits were on the Aldwych and on Earl's Court Road. Lewisham street market was also hit; one memory of this is very vivid, relating to a hit on the hospital:

> Two nights earlier the hospital had received a direct hit – on the medical block next to our nurses' home where we were sleeping… God knows how we got 200 patients out of that furnace; two were trapped, but were rescued just in time.

The deep shelters came into their own then. Juliet Gardiner explains in her book, *Wartime Britain*:

> Finally the first of the purpose-built deep shelters that had been under construction for so long admitted shelterers at Stockwell in south London on 10 July 1944. The building was 130 feet below ground and had space for 4,000 with reasonably priced canteens, lavatory and washing facilities and even arrangements for laundry.

There were also immense advantages then at having the tunnels available, such as the Ramsgate shelter which had been made after work began in March 1939. Papers had reported on that considerable achievement in positive terms:

> Emergency or no emergency, Ramsgate will be proud of its ARP tunnel... Those in authority here say that there are indications that people are looking towards Ramsgate as a place where they might spend holidays free from the anxieties that an emergency would bring. But the town is not being boosted as a haven for holiday-makers on that account – 'Health and sunshine' is still the slogan.

Nevertheless, the tunnels offered excellent safety; this was described in detail in one report:

> The scheme consists of about 2 miles of new tunnel... the new tunnel, 6ft wide and 7ft high will be cut through solid chalk at a depth of 60ft, and there will be twenty-three entrances at suitable points on open spaces.

As had been the case in the provinces, many city-dwellers left for the country. Morale was understandably way down at that point: there had been years of conventional bombing and there had been survival and resilience. But then came the rockets and the thought of more long hours in the shelters was too much for many. People trailed out into open space, often with no destination in mind. As many had reported in Hull, even a hedgerow was preferable to a place where a demonic rocket above could drop at any minute, the only warning being the loss of its power and the distinctive sound of its fall into the air over the city. Hitler and his advisors knew that smashing morale was one primary reason for a bombing campaign. With his 'rockets' he was making progress in that, so D-Day and victory could not come soon enough for Churchill. In fact, it has been suggested that Winston was considering biological warfare in retaliation against the Nazis.

Chapter 10

Their Finest Hour

'For what can war, but endless war still breed?'

John Milton

Be Prepared

In April 1941, Lord Somers was Chief Scout. The great founder of the movement, Lord Baden-Powell, had died in the midst of the conflict the previous year. Somers gave a talk in which he set out to inform people what was being done in the war by various voluntary organisations. Haydn Dimmock then spelled out exactly what the facts were for *The Times*:

> Mr F Haydn Dimmock in a brief summary of the work of Boy Scouts in the war, said that they were doing at least 178 different jobs. Last Wednesday two boys who were fire-watching from 9 o'clock to 12 o'clock, which they reported to be a comparatively quiet period, returned at 2 o'clock and for hours were extinguishing incendiary bombs. At 6.30 they went home for breakfast before setting off for their work.

In the archives of the Scout movement there is plenty of pictorial evidence that Scouts were busy assembling Morrison shelters as well as all the other duties outlined by Mr Dimmock. From the beginning of the raids, Scouts had been busy in air-raid work. Back in 1939, Somers had written to *The Times* to spell out what part his Scouts would play as their motto of 'Be prepared' took on a whole new meaning:

> Here are just a few of the duties undertaken and carried out: gas mask assembly, fitting and delivery; 24,000 were so assembled in one town;

acting as messengers for every conceivable kind of duty; distributing notices; manning first-aid posts and actual first-aid work; as patients in first-aid classes; digging trenches; bugle warnings; helping the Red Cross; telephone duty; acting as marshals for the evacuation of children; billeting arrangements for adults from London; auxiliary fire service...

This was an incredible turnaround from the communications just before the outbreak of war in which the Scouts had been told that they would not be wanted for civil defence work. Somers had commented on that at the time: 'They have hidden their disappointment as best they could and sought other means of doing their duty in doing errands for the old and infirm...'

Keith Wells, writing as part of the Postcodes Project of the Museum of London, remembered his father making their shelter:

I clearly remember dad and some neighbours installing an Anderson shelter behind part of the rockery and felling a tree which was split with metal wedges into planks to afford added strength to the roof. The 'Dog Leg' entrance led to a thin steel door. My sister and I slept on bunks whilst light and heat was provided by paraffin.

Keith was in the Scouts, and he experienced the fear of the doodlebug before he could report for duty:

One afternoon I set out to catch a bus... As I walked through the park I heard the sound of a doodlebug approaching. I then saw it flying fairly low in front of me and going from my left to right. As I had been taught, I threw myself on the ground and covered my ears with my hands.

The bomb killed five people and wounded four others.

In Greenock, Scouts became war orderlies at Greenock War Hospital. From 1942, those boys over the age of 12 became ARP messengers and fire-watchers; they even staged mock crashes to hone their skills. On one occasion they had to make a plane out of wood, tied with knots and lashings, then the troop practised bringing out the 'injured' from the plane, then first-aid skills were used on the people rescued.

Denis Perry has written memories of being with the Scouts in Croydon at the time. He has given a very clear and powerful account of their work in support of hospitals and shelters:

> As the Blitz continued, when the siren sounded we went into the maternity wards to remove new-born babies in wicker baskets and then carry them down to safety into the deep concrete air-raid shelters. The mothers were put under their bed and covered with the mattress for their protection. Also we went to wards away from the main hospital to reassure patients, and also to accompany night duty nursing staff.

The Red Cross

On the outbreak of war, there was an amalgamation of the British Red Cross Society and the Order of St. John, becoming the Joint War Organisation. Their staff worked with civilians, prisoners of war, and with the sick and wounded everywhere. The workers were to be found in hospitals, rest stations and ambulance units, and they were, of course, in shelters. The Joint War Organisation took on the responsibility of sending food parcels to prisoners abroad, as specified as permissible in the third Geneva Convention.

The first-aiders in the shelters are mentioned in all the books and they figure prominently in the oral history of the shelters. The photographic record has ample evidence of their work, and one of the most abiding images of the war is of a Red Cross nurse pinning a badge on Winston Churchill. The Red Cross workers did some amazing acts of heroism, and Betty Popkiss's story from Coventry illustrates this. She joined the St. John's Ambulance after leaving school and in October 1940 she joined an ARP post close to her home. This memory concerns a direct hit on an Anderson shelter. Betty wrote:

> It was my first job ... and that night I called into the air-raid precaution post that stood in Hen Lane, Holbrooks. As our post was only round the corner from where we lived, I used to call in most evenings to see what was going on. The bombing that night began with a shower of slow-burning incendiaries. We all ran around with sand and earth, putting them out. Then a man ran up to me and told me one was smouldering on his roof ...

Betty and others helped to put that out, but then the most awful experience came her way:

> A little girl who lived on our road ran up to me and just said 'mummy, daddy … Please …' Something was obviously terribly wrong and I told her to run on to the ARP post to get help while I dashed down the road. As I ran … I realised that a bomb had made almost a direct hit on an Anderson shelter … our neighbours, the Worthington family, were all trapped inside. Instinctively I started digging the rubble with my bare hands. It was too slow to work like that and I frantically looked around for something to use. Remarkably, I found a spade lying nearby. I remember hearing moans from inside. There was no shouting, no screams …

Help finally came and the family were brought out. Betty had been wonderfully courageous that night: she was later awarded the George Medal.

The School Caretaker

History should also spare a thought for the poor school caretakers. When the shelter was required and matters had to be taken in hand, the caretaker was called upon to act swiftly, and to do quite a lot of essential tasks. The Chief Education Officer of Birmingham made sure, in May 1940, that staff knew what was expected of them. He wrote: 'Whilst it is, of course, understood that in cases of an emergency, caretakers will use their own good judgement, the undermentioned precautions should be given preference.' His list then includes such items as:

(5) Air-raid shelters must at all times be kept in a clean condition. Hurricane lamps and sanitary arrangements must be placed in position, together with a supply of disinfectant and sawdust.

(6) After having carried out the above instructions caretakers should take cover at the earliest possible moment.

(7) Caretakers should take the first opportunity during a lull in the raid to inspect the premises, in order to ascertain whether any damage has been done and to take any necessary action. Should a fire occur which cannot be subdued by means of the apparatus installed on the school premises, steps must be taken to notify the nearest ARP or APS station.

Mass Observation

The Blitz also provided a happy hunting ground for the snoopers. In the 1930s there had been a great interest in the workers and in working-class life; they were being discovered almost as if they were living in darkest Africa, so little were their lives known by the wealthier sections of society. Therefore, when it came to the underground life of the shelters, a group called Mass Observation was only too happy to gather information on how the ordinary people behaved down there out of the light.

Mass Observation was a research outfit; it was set up in 1937 by Tom Harrisson and Charles Madge. They wanted to form what they called 'an anthropology of ourselves'. Dorothy Sheridan has explained this in her introduction to the University of Sussex archives, where these records are now held:

> Most of their early work centred around the observation of people's behaviour but they were also interested in how people wrote about their own lives – hence the diaries. During their first year of work, the organisation recruited a group of volunteers...to keep a detailed account of everything they did on the twelfth of each month.

When war broke out, this continued, and there is a stock of diaries kept by women now in the records, concerning the experience of the shelters. One typical entry is:

> Generally people feel quite pleased with the shelters saying at any rate they will give protection from splinters and shrapnel. The chief complaint was that people had to get out of their warm beds and go out in the cold, thus making illness. If you have to either die of pneumonia or get bombed I don't know which is worse.

Joyce Collins, writing in the Sussex collection, summarises one diarist of the time, Caroline Blake, in these words:

> Miss Blake's diary gives a full and detailed account of the effects of war on daily life in a village near the south coast. She tells of contacts with neighbours, some of whom ask her advice (though few seem to become close friends), the sharing or exchange of rations (four eggs for 1lb of sugar), the general strain and frequent sickness, and the somewhat casual health care...

Another summary includes this, on one June Chivers: 'She…includes accounts of conversations in shops, observations on clothes and prices…on the issue of gas masks, on the blackout and on ARP wardens. She is politically to the left…'

Margaret Bates was more concerned with the shelters: 'She gives accounts of air-raids and describes her own air-raid shelter and the arrangements made by her family for sleeping in it…She reads newspapers as regularly as time allows and always follows the war on radio…'

A typical Mass Observation report style and approach may be seen in this extract from Leonard England's writing on an air-raid in Southampton:

> Throughout Monday there was apparently a large unofficial evacuation. Two people spontaneously compared the lines of people leaving the town with bedding and prams full of goods to the pictures they had seen of refugees in Holland and Poland…Some were going to relations in outlying parts, some to shelters, preceded by their wives, who had reserved them places, and some to sleep in the open…

Mass Observation gathered information and some facts and figures: their report on all-night shelters on the Underground for 17 September 1940 includes this:

> At Piccadilly at 8 p.m. only about 2 per cent were already attempting to sleep in a sitting or doubled position. Of the others some 46 per cent were reading (mostly evening papers), some 14 per cent eating (apples seemed the favourites) and some 20 per cent of the women knitting.

They also garnered comments from those in positions of responsibility, such as this comment by a shelter marshal:

> Some of the shelterers brought a piano in and began to have noisy sing-songs after the pubs closed, keeping others awake. Failing to persuade them to be more considerate, I had to ask the local council to bring in regulations to restrict noise…They were lively times!

The meticulous writers of Mass Observation didn't miss a trick: every detail was logged.

A Star at Tilbury

In a biography of the Dean of Ely, there is a tale of the Tilbury shelter and of a character who entertained the masses:

> During the heavy Blitz of early 1941, the roads leading to the Tilbury Shelter … resounded to the tread of many thousands, who made their daily trek at sundown, when the sirens mournfully moaned their daily warning. With that sense of order which derives from the imminence of great peril, the vast crowd settled down for the night in orderly array in the great alcoves and arches or shaking down for the night on hastily improvised, nondescript beds … stoically enduring the gunfire from gun stations … But what was not familiar was the fine good humour … seeking the cause of this happy state of calm, I found it in a figure that dominated the huge assembly.

The star who was there, raising morale, was Ernie Bubley, described in Dr Bernstein's memoirs: 'On the occasions when visits to the school made it possible for me, it was a stirring experience to observe how skilfully Bubley handled his highly numerous and highly various audience.' But there was high drama one time when a bomb came down a chimney and exploded clear of the main body of the shelter and the debris went into Gower Walk. But in the aftermath, Bubley led the crowd with a rendition of 'There'll always be an England.'

Fortune Favours the Wet

Sometimes people were saved by sheer good luck and their 'shelter' was anything where they happened to be. Such was the case with a woman who was taking a bath, in her home in Poplar, when a bomb cracked into the house – a direct hit. The bomb completely demolished the house but in the explosion her bath was blown over so that it landed on top of her and the cast iron protected her. The rescuers finally reached her and she was brought out unharmed.

Mustn't Grumble

Britain being a nation of grumblers by tradition, often simply peevish and only slightly rattled by world events, there were complaints about the shelters. When an English person is moved to feel the passion of being indignant or merely tetchy, then the first move is to reach for the correspondence column contact details. If not for *The Times*, then for his local paper. Given a little column space, he or she may even add a little literary style along with the invective. Letters were about all the footnotes and details of life under a deluge of information leaflets and radio announcements – as well as a few bombs.

'Disgusted' wrote about the pain of being ignored:

Sir,

May I through the medium of your paper protest at the manner in which the corporation of Redcar are ignoring the necessity for shelters for the people of Warrenby? It has been bad enough not having gas masks for our babies. Add to this the knowledge that we have no adequate shrapnel protection and I think everyone must agree that something must be done. If they distribute the shelters we will erect them ourselves.

'Anonymous of Middlesbrough' was forceful in a similar grouch:

Sir,

It is disappointing to observe that all the work of erecting ARP shelters is taking place in the less vulnerable areas of the town, while in the Newport area on either side of the Tees Bridge, which is I would think one of the most dangerous localities, not a trench is being dug. There is quite a lot of ground here which could be used for installing trenches or shelters, and an early start would soothe the minds of people living there.

An Eccentric
Kirsten O'Neill, writing about Glasgow character A E Pickard, noted that he liked to turn heads and cause a stir. She describes his shelter:

When the war broke out Pickard built an air-raid shelter in the garden of one of his mansions. It was shaped like a cone with neon lighting all over the outside. Pickard loved the shocked looks on the faces of the air-raid wardens when they came to examine it. 'The Nazis wouldn't dare bomb A E Pickard,' he said.

In Parliament

From the very first inklings of war and bombs, the MPs were of course busy discussing every conceivable aspect of shelters. The Hansard reports are full of interminable debates on fine details, such as the question of gas curtains. This was the hot topic in Parliament on 19 September 1940:

> **Mr Mander** asked the Home Secretary to what extent gas curtains have been provided for air-raid shelter, and whether he is aware that in certain cases the police are advising against their installation?

> **Sir J Anderson**: My information is that a large majority of local authorities have taken steps to provide gas curtains, or hold them ready for installation in public shelters. I am not aware of any opposition having been offered by the police.

Others expressed a very English concern for pets:

> **Lt. Col. Sir Thomas Moore** asked the Home Secretary whether he will consider allocating a part of the public shelters to accommodate persons who are accompanied by their dogs in order to avoid danger to such individuals who refuse to leave their pets outside the shelter?

> **Sir J Anderson**: While I fully sympathise with the feelings of dog-owners, the difficulties in the way of admitting animals to public shelters are so serious that I do not feel that I could properly recommend local authorities to adopt the arrangement that my Honourable friend proposes.

Other Unsung Heroes

History has revealed numerous other people who did wonderful things in the shelter life: benefactors, selfless people, Christians and just 'good types' did amazing feats of self-sacrifice and sheer hard work down underground.

There was Olive Field, for instance: she became an MBE and was a leading figure in the Red Cross. She married Norman Field and they lived in Teesside, where there was a hospital at Lartington Hall. But in terms of her war work, she left home to work in the London shelters. Her life was the epitome of selflessness, and her MBE was awarded for services to her home area, around Barnard Castle.

Another worker in the East End shelters was Thomas Corder Catchpool. Born in 1883, he became a Quaker and became a worker with the Friends Ambulance Unit in the Great War, and in that conflict he was awarded the Mons Star. He worked in Berlin in the 1930s and at one point he was arrested by the Nazis. When war came he was a member of a committee for the abolition of night bombing, and he worked as a stretcher-bearer in the air-raid parties, being active mostly in the hospitals as well as in shelters.

Among the people who kept morale high in the shelters, Eve Maxwell-Lyte must be described. She was mainly a folk singer and was widely known and admired. During the war there was a group called the Council for the Encouragement of Music and the Arts, a prototype of the Arts Council. With them, she travelled across the land, singing in bomb-afflicted places. *The Times* praised her achievements in this work:

> She sang to audiences in air-raid shelters while the bombs fell overhead: in rest centres for the homeless in the devastated cities; at midnight and in the small hours to night shifts of factory workers; in the secret segregated hostels for munitions workers and to lonely communities of evacuees in remote villages. She journeyed, ate and slept as best she could, and worked hard. It is said that in one year she gave 360 concerts – not perhaps a matter for boasting by a professional singer in peacetime, but in those strange years a record to be proud of.

It was said of her that she was singing before she could talk.

There were countless others, anonymous or merely reticent, such as the Rev. J G Byrne, of whom the Bishop of Stepney wrote in 1951:

> He was vicar of St. Peter's, Mile End, for twenty-three years. There, in spite of advancing age, he faced the hardships and dangers of East London in wartime and was often to be found sharing with his people the communal life of the public air-raid shelters at night.

Chapter 11

In Darkest London

'For in everything he did he served the Greater Community.
Except for the War till the day he died ...'

W H Auden

S helter life became, and has stayed, a place where myths were born. Londoners had endured an ordeal beyond imagination. As time went on and more was learned about that, it became apparent that the sacrifices and trials had been profound and left deep scars. Geoffrey Field has tried to describe some of that deeper trauma: 'The strain of the raids manifested itself in a variety of less acute signs of emotional stress: anxiety attacks, extreme fatigue, eating disorders, apathy, feelings of helplessness, trembling, tics and weeping spells.' People had been living under duress for years, often developing odd beliefs and distortions of truth and of facts. Lucky charms had been popular, and strange taboos. One man said, 'After cleaning my boots we usually suffer a Blitz ...'

What happened was that Tube shelter life grasped the imagination of the press and people everywhere. Sidney Troy wrote of the Tube dwellers:

The train had its windows covered ... and when it stopped at a station and the doors opened from the centre the effect was remarkably like that of a stage ... some Tube travellers held a good deal of prejudice towards these troglodytes ... abusing them as dirty, cowardly, diseased, work shy ... or simply foreign.

Tube shelter life naturally became something with a social unit, and with a very British hue. Mass Observation did not miss the opportunity to comment and study that: 'Each shelter became more and more a self-sufficient community, with its own leaders, traditions, laws.' There was widespread planning and organising in the ranks of the 'troglodytes'. Tom Harrisson produced a piece called 'The Tube Dwellers' for that popular publication, *The Saturday Book* in 1943, in which he wrote: 'In larger shelters, spaces were allocated for smoking, recreation, nurseries, children's play and sleeping. Rules, mostly unwritten, developed about keeping gangways clear, making noise and respecting other people's space.' Shelter marshals were created. There were even shelter conferences to discuss issues and regulations.

Voluntary Organisations

In such a situation, it comes as no surprise to learn that shelters were likely to become a focus of militant thought – even the dreaded Communism might find adherents down there, some worried. Into that space therefore came the established charity and social bodies such as the Red Cross, the Salvation Army and the Women's Voluntary Service. An outstanding example of this is the work of John Groser, a socialist vicar based in Stepney, who played his part in helping the aged, finding billets and adding comfort wherever he could. Norman Ellis, from Leeds, was working in London at the time and he has written about Groser, noting that he saw him scouring the bomb-site rubble for survivors. This rare breed of man later played St. Thomas in T S Eliot's play, *Murder in the Cathedral*. But the local authorities did their bit, too; some even sending a canteen train along the Tube.

Part of 'darkest London' and shelter life was the effort to pass the time, and as already described, plenty was done to find entertainment. As well as church services, there were darts matches and story times. Yet, as is human nature, there were plenty of families who went from home to shelter, bedded down and kept themselves to themselves, treating the place as a temporary and essential respite before going home again, at least hoping they still had a home to go to.

By the summer of 1941, when there was less threat from the air, things were different. George Orwell was at a Tube at that time and he wrote:

What is most striking is the cleanly, normal domesticated air that everything now has. Especially the young married couples, the sort of homely, cautious type that would probably be buying their houses from a building society, tucked up together under pink counterpanes.

How the Tube Shelters Were Reported

Because London was most widely reported and written about, and because so many people in the arts and media wanted to write about the city or paint its people and places, the shelters were an obvious choice of subject. Before the war, there had been a type of writing that likened Britain to a place of exploration. People used phrases and terms that made readers think of uncivilised corners of the world. Magazines specialising in reports on contemporary life commissioned pieces from writers who would venture into the South Wales mining communities or into some of the less salubrious areas of the industrial towns.

The editorial of *Fact* magazine asked its readers in 1937:

> You have read, no doubt, plenty of statistical and economic accounts of this or that area or of that industry. But have you ever considered the place in which you live and the trade in which you work, with the impartial and distant eye of an anthropologist?

The *Fact* publications were really paperback books: 'Each *Fact* book contains an authoritative study of about 20,000 words in length...' ran the blurb on their flyer.

In London, a writer called Ritchie Calder was recruited into the Political Warfare branch of the Government: this meant that his duties were part of the huge propaganda machine which produced posters and leaflets for the Allies. He became well known for his book, *Carry on London*, which covered the bombings of London, Coventry and some other towns across the land. He was officially the Director of Plans and Campaigns in the Government. Calder wrote features on the shelters for the *Daily Herald* and the *New Statesman*, and he picked out characters and lively sorts of people in the underground community to write about, as in his writing on Mickey Davies, a tiny man of under 4 feet in height who was the man who controlled a large Stepney shelter in a crypt.

With Calder's pen, the shelter life became vibrant, dynamic, curious and urgently modern, as in this episode:

> Mickey the midget led me out of the shelter into the street. 'Come on,' he said, 'you haven't seen anything yet.' We went down into the crypt. An old man slept in a stone coffin, another was in use as a card table, while a navvy had levered off the lid of a third large sarcophagus and

was snoring blissfully, his deep breathing stirring up wafts of white dust ... bone dust!

Calder's account of the main shelter in Tilbury illustrates what image he was working hard to give his readers:

> Nothing like it, I am sure, could exist in the Western world. I have seen some of the worst haunts on the waterfront at Marseilles which are a byword, but they were mild compared with the cesspool of humanity which welled into that shelter in those early days. People of every type and condition, every colour and creed found their way there – black and white, brown and yellow ... When ships docked seamen would come in to roister for a few hours. Scotland Yard knew where to look for criminals out of Hell's Kitchen. Prostitutes paraded there. Hawkers paddled greasy, cold fried fish which cloyed the already foul atmosphere. Free fights had to be broken up by the police ...

There were also many pictorial representations of shelter life: Bill Brant, the photographer, came to England a few years before the war, and became involved in photo-journalism in working-class areas, and his interest in people as subjects was perfect for the images of shelter life presented to anyone with a modicum of curiosity at this time. His pictures of people in the Elephant and Castle Tube station in November 1940 show vividly the good humour and contentment which prevailed. People smile at his camera and as they lie asleep in one image, all seems to be contentment and peace.

For visual imagery, there was also Henry Moore, and he left an account in words also, of life in the Tube:

> When we got out at Belsize Park we were not allowed to leave the station because of the fierceness of the barrage. We stayed there for an hour and I was fascinated by the sight of the people camping out deep under the ground ... There were intimate little touches. Children fast asleep, with trains roaring past only yards away ...

Moore drew his shelter pictures afterwards, while the images were still new; he noted that it felt like an intrusion; after all, people dressed and undressed in the shelters; they went to the toilet and they ate and talked intimately. He drew the people in a way that ignored class and social status: they are part vision and part reality.

Tube shelter life was seen by all kinds of outside observers, from writers and painters to American servicemen and commuters, and from Mass Observation documentarists to officials in search of statistics. Of all the events of the Blitz, this element of life is indelibly pressed into the collective memory, and is indeed in some ways a part of history that has become mythic.

Crime

The well-established London resilience was everywhere in evidence, as one report put it: 'What we expected right at the beginning of the war was happening now, but people were showing fine courage … "We can take it".' The associations of tenants around the city met to discuss ways of coping; deep shelters were urgently needed, and they would have to be deep enough to withstand bombs of 500lb. Tubes were opened at night as a temporary measure.

The City police were victims too; in 1941 bombs dropped on Fore Street and Moor Lane, and Snow Hill station was hit. Constable Leonard Payne was killed as he was helping ARP wardens. Other stations were hit, including Bishopsgate and Cloak Lane. Constables Rollins and Dunnet lost their lives in the Cloak Lane bombing.

The social history around the police events was as fascinating as ever, with bizarre but very sensible measures being taken to cope with loss and disaster. A typical example was the action of a manager of a factory which had been hit and had a massive store of meat available. It needed to be eaten or be wasted, and he was given permission by the Ministry of Food to make a giant bowl of stew for the East Enders.

The city that Hitler defined as a 'decadent plutocracy' was under terrific siege; on some occasions the anti-aircraft barrage was maintained all night and the City continued to be a target, of course. The old church of St. Mary Woolnoth survived and became a place where notable churchmen gave heartening talks on religion, a haven in the midst of ruin and destruction.

But crime went on in all this chaos, and along with the ordinary everyday offences there were other police activities very much related to the war. One of these was the arrest of Dr Jagodzinski who was the London agent for *Polpress*, the news agency of Poland when occupied.

City police took him and gave him into the hands of the Military Police. The remarkable thing about that was that the Home Office knew nothing of it. This was because a law passed – the Allied Forces Act – made it imperative that all foreign deserters be handed back to the relevant authorities. It was a sad tale: Jagodzinski was a well-known academic, a man with an academic record covering positions at the universities of Paris and Liverpool. He had been working at the Slavonic School of Languages in London.

It was the cause of some trouble. The point was that the City force did not tell the Home Office, and in fact that was standard practice with the Metropolitan Police. Approaches were made to senior men in the City force and enquiries made as to how and why the arrest was made without communication.

The man was released after a hearing in front of the Polish military tribunal; he had in fact been on extended leave until the October of the year (1944) and had not reported back to his unit. No proceedings were taken against him, and the embarrassment caused to the City police was quietly forgotten. From their point of view, it appeared as an act of necessity, under law, so they had acted in a way that happens in wartime – skipping over a few rules to do something that appeared necessary.

Throughout the war years and after, one of the central issues for the police was the development of a women's police constabulary. In 1940 a circular was sent out to police authorities promoting the idea of recruiting women police. At the end of 1939 there were just 230 women constables in England; the Railway police had appointed their first women in the 1930s and the time was ripe, given wartime extreme conditions, to start work on achieving a more widespread policewomen constabulary. The first aim was for a women's auxiliary police corps. In Birmingham, the Chief Constable had already agreed to set up a training course for women; their duties were primarily seen as traffic control, driving, maintenance of police equipment and canteen work. Through modern eyes, that seems ridiculously condescending and was, of course, in line with dominant ideologies of gender at the time. No doubt male officers thought all of that quite right and fitting for the 'fairer sex'; some also thought that policing was men's work and should stay that way.

But in 1940 a writer to *The Times* pointed out that women police were needed then more than ever. The reason was that 'The help and guidance of women police would do much towards the safety of our young men and women, and their steadying presence would be a valuable factor in case of panic.' The writer also pointed out that police authorities had not responded to the Home Secretary's appeal and found it disgusting that 'such blindness and inertia' should be tolerated. By February 1941 there was a more forthright appeal for recruits. London needed women police; they were to be 'unmarried, or widows of under 35, of good character and keenness and of good physique'. They were required to be over 5 feet 4 inches tall and the pay was to be £3 2s 6d a week. There had been a case in which women officers had been notably effective: 'Two of them in particular displayed exceptional abilities at a time when London was being troubled by the outbreak of violence by members of the illegal Irish Republican Army...'

Women police were often on duty in shelters; they were also employed to work with refugees, evacuees and aliens. The police generally were at full stretch. Not only was there a large increase in crime, but they were in need of more strength. Special constables signed up, of course. In the Southampton Blitz, a new reserve constable was killed while actually inside a shelter. As Clare Leon wrote in her history of the 'specials': 'Special duties also included helping alongside the regulars and other emergency organisations such as the Civil Defence and the Red Cross... with rescue work after bombings. It was also sometimes necessary to guard against looting...'

Naturally, with communities being underground and often together for some time, crime entered the story somewhere. People may transgress when in situations of extreme trial or worry. The stories may be trivial or a little sad, such as this report from the seaside town of Skegness in 1941:

> A Skegness man and woman, both of whom were sensitive to the humiliation of going to the workhouse, were brought before the local magistrates on a charge of sleeping out in shelters and being unable to give a good account of themselves. They were separate cases, the woman being found in the High Street Public Air Raid Shelter, and the man in the Council's South Parade shelter.

When the man, John Senescall, was found in the shelter, he was asked what he was doing there. He said he was sheltering, but when taken to the station he added, 'What can I say? You know I am sleeping out!'

Stories like this are about desperation and severe poverty. But in the cities there was serious crime: looting was common, and villains took advantage of the blackout and the underground life. In January 1940, for instance, hooligans made several attacks on people in the blackout at railway stations. One report was:

> While she was waiting for a bus near Clarence Pier, Southsea, during the blackout on Wednesday night, Irene Payne, 18, of Southsea, was attacked by a man who struck her on the head four times with a weapon, believed to be a rubber truncheon. Police have been unable to trace the man or to find any weapon.

It was a time when the vulnerable were more open to attack than ever, and crimes could be committed on more opportunist occasions. In the Tube shelters, juveniles were blamed for the high rate of crimes. When people slept on the platforms, thieves would snatch their bags and run off. Young pickpockets were always operating in the shelters.

A shelter could even prove an asset for a killer. In February 1942 Evelyn Hamilton was found dead in a shelter; her handbag was stolen and she had been strangled; she turned out to be one of six victims of the man who has become known as the 'Blackout Ripper': Gordon Cummins. Evelyn was his first known victim, being found in the shelter at Montagu Place in Marylebone. Cummins was arrested after being disturbed by a delivery boy, and he left his gas mask case behind. The mask had his service number on it. He was hanged at Wandsworth on 25 June 1942.

Some of the worst offences ever committed by people are in war, of course. Even today we are familiar with images of looters at the worst disasters, stealing while bodies lie beneath the wrecks caused by bombs or hurricanes.

Afterword

'No-one can guarantee success in war, but only deserve it.'
Winston Churchill

It would be no exaggeration to say that researching these stories from sources we may best call 'living history' has made more acute the feeling that history is made of people, not ideas. Ideas and beliefs might make the buildings, but it is people and their lives that make the furniture, colour and shape of passing time. Finding out about the air-raids has, I hope, destroyed some fixed ideas and stereotypes. With the passing of time, we have laughed at the periods of austerity we know as the 'war years' and the '50s which felt the deprivations of life in the long aftermath of the conflict. For the younger generation, *Dad's Army* and *'Allo 'Allo!* have had an impact on their impressions.

Yet, in spite of the sitcom stereotypes involving lines such as 'Don't get granddad started on the war', a closer understanding of those years is now emerging. For too long the period has been dominated by the military history enthusiasts: quite understandably, men who watch hours of television war programmes every day and eagerly seek out memoirs by ex-servicemen at the local library, the war against Germany, Italy and Japan in those dark years became central to their whole lives. Some would never talk about 'their war'. But on the Home Front, the untold stories have now flowed freely and the urgency to express the experience has rivalled the tales of tanks and warships.

Life in the air-raid shelters has left us with images of absolute extremes. These two memories illustrate just how extreme the oral history chronicles can be. First, Mary Harrison writing for the Wartime Memories Project, about a direct hit on Wilkinson's shelter:

My two uncles described the scene as something they would never forget for the rest of their lives. They were lined up outside the shelter passing bodies, or in some cases pieces of bodies, as they were being dug out from the rubble. My Uncle Peter was one of the lucky ones. His wife went to the shelter but was told it was full so she went somewhere else…

Now a memory from Billy Docherty: 'In the shelter people were singing and the children were making a noise and one old lady would say, "Wheesht, wheesht, they'll hear ya!" People didn't get much sleep.'

Memories came to me from people who were children in the war of course; so many stories were about adults from a viewpoint below. Plenty of tales were of fathers digging and mothers singing or cuddling. The perspectives from older people, those who were young people in the war, and some who played a part in official capacities, have a special quality – one of lifting burden.

These scraps of memories show just how different the tales can be from experiences of trauma. Yet somehow, for all the horrible events, air-raid shelters provide subject for discussion that usually leads to smiles. In most cases, what happened inside the shelters was more the human comedy than high tragedy. Yes, there were direct hits, but they were rare. Most people who responded to my call for stories wanted to relate the footnotes of history: the laughs, the ironies and the farce, rather than try to explain the massive events.

When I first conceived of how to assemble this material, I had no idea just how massive the response for information would be. There were letters, messages, pictures, original documents and photos. But there were also the phone calls: so many people in their 80s have no computers, and so I made calls and then that entailed listening to the most heartbreaking stories on the phone. Voices came across to me as they had done over the years, firm and poignant memories of loss, parting and sheer dark feelings of despair. People spoke plainly about friends dying next to them, and of bodies being brought out of the wreckage. Yet there were also stories of absolute farce, bizarre tales from the human comedy, with the spirit of victory and survival to the fore.

The Blitz, in one sense, has been over-told. By that I mean that anniversaries have been and gone; the heritage industry has fastened on to the importance of retrieval of these stories, and schoolchildren have read, listened and learned with awe and wonder at what their antecedents had to endure. Yet, the stories are told with such urgency, and with the voice of blandness, as the pain has been lived through for so long, the danger is that the new generation will not listen attentively. The voices have become more insistent and sonorous, and so it becomes more difficult every day to look to the happier side of the shelter life, though there undoubtedly was a wonderful camaraderie in many places. The overall situation was that some people were in public shelters from sheer necessity, and they had no desire to gel and integrate or join in community singing or bingo; while others relished the shelter culture and looked forward to it. For children it was an adventure; for some adults it was a release from routine, and for professionals it was just another responsibility. But everyone was bound in the shackles of war and they shared a common enemy in Mr Hitler, whose face was caricatured on every available space and in most publications. There was a strong feeling of living on the edge: that each day might be your last. Most people had loved ones somewhere else across the globe, and many did not fully understand the politics of it all. The only fact that mattered was that England was under threat and that it was unthinkable that there was a future in which everyone would be speaking German and be classified as 'an Aryan race'.

We know a lot about the human stories, but the drier, factual material is in academic history books. For instance, in 1952 someone calculated the cost of all the shelter construction. The Civil Estimates for what was known as Class III 'Home Department, Law and Justice' recorded that £83,000 was spent on acquiring and maintaining air-raid shelters in the years 1952–53. Shelters were being kept – as shuddering thoughts of possible nuclear war were acknowledged. Only three years before, local authorities had been asked by the Government to conduct a survey of wartime shelters. At that time, the advice was that:

In planning for communal shelters … it must be remembered that unframed buildings within a wide radius of an atomic bomb burst would collapse, and if their basements had been used as shelters the resulting rescue problems might be beyond the resources available.

One conclusion has struck me in doing the research: the body of material which constitutes the oral history of the shelters is peculiarly clamorous

– it is as if the voice of memory has been dumb in so many quarters, and when asked, the buried memories have surfaced, but they have done so in such a way that people struggle for the vocabulary, while appealing for others to corroborate the scale of the enormity they knew.

The template example of this was as I sat in an audience at the Hull History Centre, after listening to a woman on film recall her time in shelters and in bomb-strafed streets. A man who had been sitting quietly began to speak when questions were asked for. His story was enough to sustain a novel of the most angst-ridden kind. This man had started walking away into the farmlands of Holderness, what Philip Larkin called 'the end of England' – clearly suffering from the trauma of the incendiaries and the gunfire of the ack-acks. He wandered aimlessly, unaware what he was doing apart from the fact that he wanted to be eventually on a farm, as he thought that would have been safe. Listening, I had the feeling that he had not told anyone this before.

If we see the experience of being bombed and sitting in the dark, wondering if the home will be there next morning, as something that is always with us, somewhere across the world, then an attempt at understanding may begin, but there is a danger in generalising. As I write this, there are bombs across Beirut and Afghanistan. But the people under the Nazi bombers had a unique experience, just as those in the places mentioned do now. The stories collected here go some small way towards making that experience approachable and significant.

Hopefully, the foregoing tales and pictures will do something to offer a fresh bundle of war stories. All that may be said with confidence is that all my correspondents here have supplied another archive in print, another assembly of stories that will have a kind of immortality. The pain lies in the spaces between the words. Silence is a major element in suffering of course, as some experience is beyond the capacity of words at times. I listened on the phone to thousands of words, but I also had the silences, and they spoke volumes.

The only type of shelter without its oral history appears to be the individual one: from early in the war a company called Constructors of Erdington, Birmingham, produced a shelter called the 'Consol'. This was for 'key personnel' and they supplied these for guards at Buckingham Palace and St. James's Palace. We have a massive archive of stories on Andersons, Morrisons, underground and brick public shelters. We have tales from church crypts, coal cellars and company basements, but nothing from the soldiers encased in the Consols. They were a conical shape, glossy like something from *Dr Who* and the illustrations of them show a military type exiting, dressed like a space invader.

Britain now has a vast historical heritage industry, and people are applying for grants across the land, to spend on reclaiming the collective memory; other wars have succeeded the Blitz of Hitler's war, but none has really had the depth of impact of those years in which people were tried and tested every day, for what must have seemed like an eternity of waiting, with no guarantee of success.

Yet, as well as the looking back, it is important that today's young people not only see and experience 'bomb culture' of those years in text, but also use and explore the physical space: an example is the work done by Fereshte Moosavi at the University of Plymouth, a woman who has had personal experience of wartime shelters in the Iran-Iraq war. She told the press, when working on a shelter behind the North Hill campus at Plymouth: 'I wanted to give this particular shelter a new function and more importantly make sure that the memories of those who used them were not forgotten.' She has used the shelter as a place for her public art, creating transparent photographic images on the walls underground.

Optimistically, I can see the kind of event held by the Hull History Centre on the 'citizens' experience of war' becoming something we want to see more often. There is a crying need for a forum across the country on this area of memory reclamation. There is some sense in finding ways to place these stories in sites other than the nostalgia magazines. If nothing is done to make a national database, as in the Sound Archive projects at the British Library, then what will happen is that tapes and CDs will gather dust on a shelf somewhere. I once worked on a feature concerning Polish immigrants in Kirklees. At the town library, the best resource I found was not something in print: it was a collection of audio tapes based on interviews with older people in the area. The respondents had experienced the war in Eastern Europe; many had fought with the Allies at battles such as Monte Cassino, and they had all had to come and settle in a foreign country, learn the language and find work. Many talked of themselves as 'the invisible people' in Yorkshire. The last thing anyone would want would be for our war memories to have a similar destination in terms of storage and use.

That kind of unity and empathy, between people today who cower under bombings, and those with memories of past shelter life, is one of our great hopes for the future: something crossing boundaries and provoking thought. The tales from the shelters sometimes present a smile in the face of adversity, and that, finally, will be the hallmark of the ultimate triumph of the Home Front people against the bombers.

Two Final Images

Two images will lodge forever in my mind from all the material I have used and read:

One: Cleaning the Doorstep

The first is a small but powerful insight by Doris Scott who lived in Canning Town in East London: 'Once, as I was leaving my shelter and coming back to my house, those all around were bomb blasted and I saw this woman cleaning the front doorstep of her demolished house as if it were business as usual.'

Two: The Old Couple

In Susan Briggs' book, *Keep Smiling Through*, there is a photo of a couple sitting on two chairs beside a shattered home, a window hanging out precariously behind them. He wears a hat and scarf and has a Union Jack on one knee. She wears a fur-trimmed overcoat and hat and she leans across, her head to his chest. She sleeps, probably with exhaustion, and he lays his head over hers, a crease on one of his cheeks as if he smiles or says something consoling to her.

These two contrasting images depict what is common to all wars: the odd, illogical purposes people have in simply carrying on, in situations where routine is actually the greatest comfort; then the touching, intensely human act of expressing comfort and affection in the most extreme circumstances. What both images say is that normality – whatever we think of as that – fundamentally exists in how we act towards each other and to what extent we act rather than think, discuss and philosophise. Both images show actions: one from person to person and the other from a person to the last remnant of the little world that has been made for her to inhabit.

Thanks and Acknowledgements

This book has been put together from dozens of private archives as well as from a random batch of voices from oral history. I thought it was going to be a process of dredging, but I was wrong: it has simply been a case of editing and shaping a mass of material, so the thanks due are many and varied. Although there is a massive library in print and on film of the Second World War, the material on life in shelters has been patchy, and has been best preserved by individual enthusiasts, although there have been special exhibitions over the years. My sources have therefore been a mix of piecemeal anecdotes and collected oral history projects.

The research and preparatory work for *Air-Raid Shelters* entailed gathering thousands of stories from across England, and the following list is a summary of most of the sources and help I had. My apologies go to anyone whose name has been unintentionally omitted here.

There are also people who, though not widely known outside their native places, played very important roles in the planning of shelters and other precautions in the build-up to the war, and outstanding among these is Sir Leo Schultz of Hull (Lord Mayor there from 1942–43). This work is fittingly dedicated to his memory.

Hundreds of people have helped with the work for this book. Responses to my letters asking for anecdotes, memories and pictures exceeded all expectations. Thanks for material and for memories go to John Baker, Neil Farrell, Daniel Fiander, Carl Mallett, Maureen Owen, Frank Dolman, Vincent McDonagh, David Wilcockson, Edwin Gardner, Fred Common, Jim Warren, Geoffrey Smith, Colin Wilson, Norman Backhouse, Pat Bishop, J Walsh, Neil McCallum, Roy Westall, Jack

Sammons, Brian Elliott, Peter Langham, Frank Rawlinson, Mr Mike Hollingdale of the 351st Bomb Group Reunion Association, staff at Hemswell antiques centre, Joan Wilkinson and T Geraghty. Robert Matthews provided one of the best mystery stories, in the tale of his brother.

Many memories had to be told over the phone, as several correspondents had no computer facilities. Listening to accounts of bomb blasts and the deaths of relatives was not exactly fun, and I have to express a debt of gratitude to those people who shared stories of loss and trauma with me in that way.

An honourable mention goes to George Whitehead, who reminded readers of *BBC History Magazine* that Hull was bombed, with over 1,200 deaths as a result of those raids (letter printed in the issue for February, 2010). Following that up, Allison Coggan has to be thanked for helping in my appeal to readers of the *Hull Daily Mail* to give me their stories. They certainly responded in full.

Helpful organisations have been Hartlepool Library Service, Hull Local History Library, The Greenwich Heritage Centre, University of Plymouth and the various local newspaper items from websites quoted in the text.

My mother, Joyce Wade, supplied some Leeds memories, and several writers and historians contributed pictures and anecdotes.

Special mention must be made of Jean Gough, Derek Sprake and Ben Sansum, who provided substantial material for my use, and similarly, thanks to Dennis Grout, who provided a copy of the *Look North* film on the Hull Blitz in which he figures.

I appreciate the assistance of the editors of *Best of British*, *The Dalesman* and *Down Your Way* magazines, and the editors at the *Hull Daily Mail*, *The Liverpool Echo* and the *Sheffield Star* in helping to disseminate my appeals for stories. In particular, I have to thank all the following who responded to Allison Coggan's feature with stories: Frank Evenden, Brenda Cooper, Ben Adamson, Janet Fraser, Olive Tebbatt, Betty Levesley, Clifford Dalton, Cheryl Rickles, Dennis Grant, Kenneth Woodhouse, Pauline Harmer, Eileen Webster (née Dewhurst), Trevor Jones, Evelyn Bateman, R A Atkinson, Pauline Edmonds, Jean Billany, Bill Biglin, Penny Wright, Alan Dent, June Broadley, Gilbert Austin, Judith Russell, David Peat, Rich Avery, John Roberts, Brian Cook, Margaret Andrew, Mike and Jean Baker, Ron Atkinson, Alison North, Jean Sleath and Eric Wright.

Without Brian Callan's help there would have been no story about Roddy the dog, so thanks to Brian for that, and to Trevor Jones, whose mother's diary of the Hull Blitz is an invaluable record. Brian Clarke also kindly supplied copies of his father's memoirs and other material.

My Plymouth informants included Miss Jeanette Hipsey, who kindly gave me anecdotes and valuable printed material. Without her input, there would have been no feature on the Favata memorial at the University of Plymouth.

For the Hull stories, special thanks go to David Peat and the material on his father, Raymond Peat, whose chronicles are recorded at the Imperial War Museum.

Stephen Wood kindly gave permission for material from the Clifford Road archive to be used here.

Acknowledgements for photographs and images:
Tommy Hart for his picture of the shelter at Herringthorpe; images from the Lincolnshire Archives, courtesy of Lincolnshire County Council, at the Illustrations Index; drawings by Vicky Schofield; Jonathan Ginn for the shelter marker photos; David Peat for the picture of his father, and for the copy of his taped memories. Thanks to Ben Sansum for the photos of his 1940s material and locations.

Pictures from *The London Archaeologist* feature are by courtesy of the Hendon and District Archaeology Society; thanks to Don Cooper for arranging that use, and to Keely Lead.

Staff at the Hull History Centre kindly arranged for the pictures from the Hull Blitz to be used, particularly Christine Brown and Isaac Acheampong.

Thanks to Steve Johnson of Plymouth, and his excellent site, cyber-heritage.co.uk. Steve introduced me to the phenomenon of 'urbexing' – something that is helping to bring shelters into prominence with younger people too, as they explore cityscapes. Shelters, just as much as old dungeons or castles, are now being explored with a sense of mystery and younger people are learning about Britain at war through that hobby. In addition, the site for Subterranea Britannica was extremely useful.

R J Maxwell kindly supplied the photograph of his father's invention, the 'bed-type' shelter, made by Robert Morris Ltd., of Farnworth, near Bolton.

Credit also to Edmund Forte for his family history material on Exeter, and to the *Living Here* website project in Exeter, and to the related material from Roy Huxtable.

Becky Wallower of *The London Archaeologist* was very helpful with the Edgware School story.

For the Colchester records, thanks to the diaries of E J Rudsdale: blogposts on the 'Homefront' website cited below.

Daniel Fiander has to be thanked for helping to deliver his grandfather, Gordon's, memories and drawings of the Sheffield bombings. Similar family archives and other material from Dennis Grout and the *Look North* documentary on his life and the reunion with family added something special.

There are countless other sources of various small gobbets of information which proved to be useful, and these have been acknowledged in the text. One special mention must be made for David Carney, who contributed the poem to the Anderson shelter.

Finally, thanks go to Isabel Atherton: this would never have been conceived and written without her involvement.

Bibliography

Books

Ackroyd, Peter, *London: The Biography* (Vintage, 2001)

Arthur, Max, *Forgotten Voices of the Second World War* (Ebury Press, 2005)

Arup, O N, *Design, Cost, Construction and Relative Safety of Trench, Surface, Bomb-Proof and Other Air-Raid Shelters* (Concrete Publications, 1939)

Briggs, Susan, *Keep Smiling Through: the Home Front 1939–45* (Book Club Associates, 1975)

Calder, Angus, *The People's War: Britain 1939–45* (Cape, 1969)

Carey, John, *William Golding: the Man who Wrote Lord of the Flies* (Faber and Faber, 2009)

Chamberlain, E R, *Life in Wartime Britain* (Batsford, 1972)

Clifford, Sue and King, Angela, *England in Particular* (Hodder and Stoughton, 2006)

Davies, John, *A History of Wales* (Penguin, 2007)

Dudgen, Piers, *Our East End* (Headline Review, 2008)

Eliade, Mircea, *Autobiography* (University of Chicago Press, 1988)

Gardiner, Juliet, *Wartime Britain 1939–1945* (Headline, 2004)

Gardiner, Juliet, et al, *The 1940s House* (Channel 4 Books, 2000)

Garnett and Richard Weight, *Modern British History: The Essential A-Z Guide* (Pimlico, 2004)

Gaskin, M J, *Blitz: the Story of 29th December, 1940* (Faber and Faber, 2005)

Geraghty, T, *A North-East Coast Town: the story of Kingston upon Hull in the 1939–1945 Great War* (Hull Academic Press, 2002)

Glinert, Ed, *East End Chronicles* (Penguin, 2005)

Gregory, Kenneth, *The First Cuckoo: Letters to The Times since 1900* (Unwin, 1978)

Hawthorne, Jenny, *East End Memories* (Sutton, 2006)

Home Office, *Air Raid Precautions: Directions for the Erection and Sinking of the Galvanised Corrugated Steel Shelter* (Home Office, 1939)

Lewis, Jon E, *The Mammoth Book of How it Happened in Britain* (Robinson, 2001)

Longmate, Norman, *How We Lived Then: a History of Everyday Life During the Second World War* (Hutchinson, 1971)

Lucas, Edgar, *Practical Air Raid Protection* (Jordan and Sons, 1939)

Mass Observation Diaries: An Introduction published by the Mass Observation Archive, University of Sussex, and the Centre for Continuing Education, University of Sussex (1991)

Ministry of Home Security, *How to Put Up Your Morrison Shelter* (Ministry of Home Security, 1941)

Ministry of Home Security, *Shelter at Home* (HMSO, 1941)

Moss, Alan and Skinner, Keith, *The Scotland Yard Files* (National Archives, 2006)

Orwell, George, *Diaries* (ed. Peter Davison), (Harvill Secker, 2009)

Orwell, George, *The Collected Essays, Journalism and Letters of George Orwell*, 4 vols. (Penguin, 1970)

Priestley, J B, *Postscripts* (Heinemann, 1946)

Quinn, Tom, *London's Strangest Tales* (Portico, 2008)

Readers' Digest: Secrets and Stories of the War (*Readers' Digest*, 1963)

Sprake, Derek, *Men of Chale* (Coco Design, 2006)

Van Young, Sayre, *London's War: a Traveller's Guide to World War II* (Ulysses Press, 2008)

White, Jerry, *London in the Twentieth Century* (Vintage Books, 2008)

Articles in Journals and Magazines

Charman, Terry, 'How Britain Learnt to Live on Rations', *Independent* 15.1. 2010 pp. 30–31

Cross, Eddie, 'Air Raids, Recycling, Radio and Rationing', *Down Your Way* (Issue 145, January 2010) pp. 34–37

Davies, Barbara, 'Take Cover', *Daily Mail: The Blitz Issue* 10 April 2010, pp. 10–11

Field, Geoffrey, 'Nights Underground in Darkest London: The Blitz 1940–1941', *Cercles 17* pp. 181–217

Hicks, David, 'We're all on the Frontline now after Deadly Air Raid', *Down Your Way* (Issue 142, October 2009) pp. 49–53

Kynaston, David, *Family Britain 1951–57* (Bloomsbury, 2009)

Leon, Clare, 'Special Constables in the First and Second World Wars', *Journal of the Police History Society* No.7, 1992, pp. 1–41

Moshenska, Gabriel, 'Unearthing an Air Raid Shelter at Edgeware Junior School', *The London Archaeologist* (Summer, 2007)

Nichols, Beverley, 'I Found Peace in an Air Raid', *Daily Sketch*, (29 August 1940)

Osman, Arthur, 'Midland Diary', *The Times* 23 September 1980, p.14

Local History Publications/Heritage
Hull History Centre archive for World War II
University of Plymouth: *Portland Square Memorial Sculpture* 2009
Wright, Jim, *Skegness at War Vol. I 1939–40* (the author, no date)

Private Archives and Collections
Brian Cook: *Walter Ernest Cook collection*
Trevor James: *Personal diary and logbook of Vera James*
Derek Sprake: *Men of Chale*: additional papers to his book of that title

Periodicals and Newspapers
Series: *The Daily Telegraph World War II Eye Witness collection* (2009)
BBC History Magazine
British Medical Journal
Daily Sketch
Daily Telegraph
Evening Herald
History Today
Hull Daily Mail
Local Historian
Military History
Milwaukee Journal
Police Journal
Shields Evening News
Stockport Times East
The Local Historian
The Times
The War Illustrated

Recorded Material
Imperial War Museum recording: Mr Peat
The World at War series

Websites
http://uktv.co.uk/yesterday/item/aid/633217
http://wwar2homesfront.blogspot.com
www.bmj.com/cgi
www.culture24.org.uk/history
www.durham–pa.go.uk
www.edmundforte.co.uk
http://hansard.millbanksystems.com/commons/1940/sep/19/air-raid-shelters

www.history.ac.uk/ihr/Focus/War/LondonCivil.html
www.holyheadmaritimemuseum.co.uk
www.irishstatutebook.ie/1940/en/0215.html
www.jfsalumni.com/drbernsteinmemoirs/?disp_feature=OsHIoN
http://londonist.com/2009/01/london_v2_rocket_sitesmapped.php
www.mayflowersteps.co.uk/plymouth/theblitz.html
www.museumoflondon.org.uk/postcodes/places/E18/stories/CAT111.html
www.openwriting.com/archives
www.plimsoll.org/Southampton/Southanmptonatwar/southamptonsblitz/default.asp
www.plymouthdata.info/Second%World%20War-1941-Blitz.htm
www.recollectionsofwwii.co.uk
www.redcross.org.uk
www.spartacus.schoolnet.co.uk
www.tynelives.org.uk/war/factory/images
www.wandsworth.go.uk/info/200064/local_history_and_heritage/122/wartime_vo
www.westallswar.org/archives
www.whatsonsouthwest.co.uk

Index